KINTSUGI

BEAUTIFULLY BROKEN

ALLISON R. MICHELS

ISBN: 979-8-32646-862-8

Imprint: LAUNCH, LLC

KINTSUGI:

Kintsugi is the Japanese art of putting broken pottery pieces back together with gold — built on the idea that in embracing flaws and imperfections, you can create an even stronger, more beautiful piece of art. Every break is unique and instead of repairing an item like new, the 400-year-old technique actually highlights the "scars" as a part of the design. Using this as a metaphor for healing ourselves teaches us an important lesson: Sometimes in the process of repairing things that have broken, we actually create something more unique, beautiful and resilient.

By Vaneetha Risner

I dedicate this book to all the amazing women
in my life that inspired me to understand
it's okay to be beautifully broken.

Dear Friend,

I wrote this book to help you heal.
You are stronger than you know.
You are more resilient than you realize.
You are worthy of love.
You deserve peace.
I believe in you.
You have got this!

All My Love,
Allison

CONTENTS

INTRODUCTION

*May God bless you, keep you, and may
His face shine upon you, offering you
hope and strength on your journey.*

I n July 2022 my life shattered. I had endured the painful
loss of my marriage, what I once saw as a "perfect" family,
my dream home, several close friends, and even my sense of
self-worth.

I found myself in a place where it seemed like there was
nothing left, and the path to recovery felt uncertain and
daunting. The future appeared bleak, and I struggled to
envision anything positive on the horizon.

During this period, my confidence was nonexistent. I cried
daily, my self-esteem was in tatters, stress had impacted
my appetite, and simply making it through each day was a
monumental challenge.

You might wonder why I'm sharing this deeply personal
and difficult moment. It's because I believe that part of
our journey in life is to traverse these trying, often painful,
moments and then share our experiences. Sometimes, these

moments are our lowest points, the ones we'd rather bury deep within us, the ones that fill us with shame or a knot in our stomach. To this day, tears well up in my eyes when I recall some of the intense experiences I endured that year. Someone once told me, "Allison, it's like you are living a nightmare." Sadly, they were right.

Imagine facing all your worst fears, and even those you never imagined could come true, becoming a harsh reality in your life: lies, deception, excruciating pain, destruction, and baseless accusations.

You find yourself questioning whether this nightmare is real, waking up day after day only to realize that it is indeed your reality, a reality you never wanted. In that moment, you face a choice: to run and hide or to confront the demons head-on. No one else can make this choice for you. There's no road map for navigating this kind of trauma and pain. To be honest, I don't think most people experience such intense trauma in the way and timing that I did. I wouldn't wish this on anyone.

But I chose to confront the nightmare head-on.

This all happened on my prayer bench, roughly halfway up Rib Mountain in Wausau. I've been praying on that bench for years. On that day, I screamed at God for help. I was furious about the suffering my children and I had endured. I was devastated and simply yearned for a life filled with peace and love.

In that moment, one of my lowest points, I was angry with God. I grappled with how a supposedly benevolent God could allow such pain and hardship into my life. How could a God who loves me not shield me from this excruciating pain, so deep and intense that I doubted whether I could ever recover?

"Why, God, WHY!?" I cried out.

Sitting on that bench, tears streaming down my face, my body wracked with pain and despair, I was grateful that no one passed by on the trail at that moment. I was experiencing a complete breakdown, and I couldn't fathom anyone witnessing it.

I'm not sure how long I cried, yelled, and pleaded with God, but once I had emptied myself of all the hurt, anger, and burning questions, I wiped my tears and walked away.

I left all my pain at that bench, letting God take charge. I let go and surrendered.

As someone who had always been a self-proclaimed control freak, I realized I no longer had any control over the situation. All I could do was lean on God's strength to lead me and my children toward a new life.

I reached a point of pure surrender, not because I wanted to, but because I had no other choice. I hadn't chosen the circumstances in my life, and I couldn't begin to regain control of the situation. I knew only God could help me. So, on that bench, I gave it all to Him to figure out. I prayed in a way I had never prayed before. I was desperate, in need of even the slightest glimmer of hope and a plan.

As I walked away from that bench, a warm tingling washed over my entire body. A lightness filled my heart, my tears ceased, and the knot in my stomach dissolved. I knew, deep within me, that I would be alright. The journey of healing had begun.

This is my healing journey, not intended as a professional guide since I am not a medical professional. It's merely meant to share my experience. Will it help you? Perhaps. I hope so. My wish is that if you're currently facing something in your life that seems insurmountable, you'll find some inspiration for your own healing journey. Take what resonates with you and leave what doesn't.

DAY 1

*"God doesn't want you to change; He
wants you to become more of who you
are."*

—*Grandma Char*

At times, when we set out to mend things that are broken, we unintentionally craft something even more unique, exquisite, and resilient.

Today, I woke up at the age of 40, feeling happier than I've been in years. My heart brims with love, not just for the wonderful people in my life, but also for myself. I sense a profound tranquility and contentment that I've never known before. I've grown more secure in my identity, understanding that I am guided and loved.

Today, I embark on this journey of writing my sixth book, following one of the most challenging seasons in my life. I've encountered adversity, humiliation, shame, pain, change, hurt, destruction, and false accusations beyond what I ever imagined possible. While I may share fragments of that story, my intention for this book is to serve as a guide, helping you navigate your own pain and hurt in a way that awakens the uniqueness, beauty, and resilience within you. Discovering your true self amidst life's trials has the power to transform you into what you were always meant to be.

In a conversation with my Grandma Char about this concept, I realized that all my previous books, courses, trainings, and speeches were rooted in the idea that you must change yourself to "become" who you want to be. However, over the past year, I've come to understand that you don't need to change who you are; rather, you need to become more of who you were created to be. Embrace your quirks, your laughter, your silliness, your voice, your gifts, your talents— all that makes you uniquely you. These are the facets you need to embrace because they define who you are and how you're meant to share your gifts with the world. That is your purpose.

FEELING BROKEN:

I was hiking the mountain near my home when I paused to sit on my prayer bench. I broke down in tears—my heart ached, my body throbbed, and I cried harder than I thought possible. The despair and pain had shattered me. Overwhelming shame and guilt enveloped me, and the swirling questions left me in confusion.

I sat on the bench, utterly alone, shattered and broken.

Being in a state of brokenness is a terrible place to find oneself. It feels hopeless and agonizing, as though a dark cloud has cast its shadow over your heart and thoughts. During this period of brokenness, I wondered if I would ever laugh again. Could I wake up without a sense of dread and pain? Could I make it through a day without succumbing to anguish? Could I experience a day when I didn't have to call my best friend in tears? To cope with this pain and hurt, I had to compartmentalize my life into tiny, manageable pieces, knowing that anything more would bury me.

The pain and hurt became my new normal, and crying became a way of life. Confronting life's difficult facets had become a reality I detested.

Let me share a little about myself when I'm at my best, when I'm happy. I'm kind of awesome and funny. I radiate vibrancy and laughter. My attitude toward life is sunny and optimistic. In fact, my daughter's middle name is HOPE, chosen because I believe in the enduring power of hope. This is the true essence of who I am.

Yet, during this season of brokenness, I lost her—the positive, hopeful part of myself. I lost hope.

Have you ever been there? Have you ever been dragged into the depths of despair, where the pain and hurt make it hard to breathe, let alone feel anything positive?

If your answer is no, then perhaps this book isn't for you. But if you've experienced or are currently experiencing this raw, intense pain, then you understand. You know! I know, and you know...

The place we're going is that space of knowing, where the pain and hurt run so deep that you wonder if life will ever improve. The knowing that all you yearn for is to feel better and happier. The knowing that you deserve such a life and love, but you question if it's even possible.

That's where we're headed. Are you ready? Your broken pieces are part of the beautiful kaleidoscope of your life.

DAY 2:
SEEK ASSISTANCE

My word for the year was "receive." To truly receive, you often need to seek help. I'll be honest; I've never been comfortable asking for help. I grew up as an only child, fiercely independent. In third grade, I'd ride my bike to the library to check out books, fill up a bag, and try to ride back home, occasionally toppling over my bike. I was determined to figure out life on my own.

Reaching a point in my life where I couldn't figure it all out was painful. As my life unraveled, I distinctly recall cautiously approaching my best friend for help and advice. Simply admitting to someone that my world wasn't perfect felt uncomfortable.

I remember calling my friend and pouring out everything I was going through—the pain, the hurt, the lies, all of it. I bared my soul to her and waited... In truth, I half-expected her to respond with something snarky or unkind. Not because she was like that, but because that was my assumption about sharing the messy parts of my life. The old me might have been judgmental. But she wasn't. She listened with compassion. She leaned into my pain, and her tone of voice conveyed how much she cared.

Another pivotal moment in my healing journey followed that first conversation where I asked for help. I realized that I could trust others to support me. I grasped that pain is a shared human experience, and although she hadn't felt my pain exactly as I had, she could empathize with it. She leaned into my suffering and helped me understand that it was a natural response to having the life I cherished torn apart for me and my children. The destruction was overwhelming, and it was okay to feel sad, angry, and frustrated about it. It was okay to confide in someone else about what I was enduring. It was the first time I had truly done that—told my truth and asked for help.

Reflecting on the idea of seeking assistance, I've come to realize that the reason I had never done it before is because it feels incredibly vulnerable. Vulnerability requires openness, and when you open up, there's the potential for even more hurt, which can be frightening. Yet, as I opened up to my friend, I repeatedly found myself supported and loved. I felt equipped to face the darkness that surrounded me because I didn't have to do it all alone anymore. I was waging a battle to reclaim my life, and that battle, at times, tore at my heart. It was scary, exhausting, and often overwhelming.

But then, one day, something remarkable happened—I didn't cry.

Not even once!

Naturally, I called my friend. "Hey, I didn't cry today!" I exclaimed. She celebrated this small milestone with me. Day by day, little by little, I leaned into the hope that each new day would be a little brighter. My friend infused hope into my life. On one occasion during my healing journey, I visited her at her home. Overwhelmed by the weight of the pain I had been carrying, I broke down. I laid on a couch in her office as she prayed over me and massaged my back with her massage gun. She placed crystals all around me. I left that room feeling lighter than I had in many months.

Healing takes various forms. Finding grounding during times of stress is profoundly healing. Grounding can encompass activities such as walking outside barefoot, using crystals, meditation, or deep breathing. I began meditating daily with my Calm app. Those meditative moments offered a respite from my stressful thoughts, even if only for 10 minutes. In those 10 minutes, I realized that my thoughts weren't me; they were something I could observe. I also understood that my emotions weren't me either; I could witness them and let them flow through me. I didn't suppress them; I acknowledged the feelings, named them, and allowed myself to fully experience them. Many times, this led to tears as a way to release pent-up emotion.

Seeking help was transformative in my healing process because it taught me that I could rely on others for support. Knowing that you have support in life means the world. Having even one person who truly cares and shows up during your moments of hurt is invaluable. However, it's important to note that staying perpetually stuck in a place of pain for years is too much. When I asked for help, I did it in a way where I wasn't angry or resentful; I was seeking loving guidance. I wasn't immobilized; I was open to change and open to healing. I also opened my heart to viewing life through a different lens. One mantra that aided me was "I choose to see love." Opting to see love in moments of pain allowed me to look beyond my immediate circumstances and connect with the hope that positive things could still happen in my life. I began journaling each morning, jotting down all the beautiful things I was grateful for. Initially, it was challenging because my life was falling apart, but I searched for the good. I'd write about having coffee, my children's laughter, my friends and family, the sunshine, my health, and my dog. Every day, I scoured my life for more things to be grateful for. Throughout the day, I actively sought out the good. When I found it, I'd remember it for my nightly journaling session. Be on the lookout for goodness in life, and it will reveal itself. Seek out small blessings every day. When you do this, you'll begin to see goodness everywhere, and you'll feel an overwhelming sense of gratitude every day.

Recently, I sat at my birthday party, looking around and feeling an intense sense of gratitude for that moment and for the incredible people in my life. Appreciation brings peace.

So, my message to you is simple: Ask for help and be willing to receive it!

DAY 3:
PERSEVERE

L ast night, I had a conversation with a friend from high school. We first crossed paths in the freshman year during volleyball practice, and our friendship has endured ever since. She knows me inside and out, and I know her just as well. Together, we've navigated numerous life milestones: graduations, heading off to college, buying our first homes, getting married, welcoming babies into the world, securing our first jobs, dealing with the loss of loved ones, and everything in between.

As I updated her on my life and she shared her own, she paused and said something that struck me: "Allison, do you realize how much you've grown in this past year? I remember talking to you around this time last year when you were separated and had filed for divorce. You had to rebuild everything in your life—a house, a car, a job, even a relationship."

Everything in my life has undergone a transformation in just one year, right down to the pajamas I wear! It might sound trivial, but I consciously decided to trade in my worn-out T-shirts and pajama pants for matching, stylish pajamas. This small act helped me recognize that I was worthy of something as simple as fancier sleepwear. Each night, as I prepared to sleep, I'd think about how cute they were and how grateful I was that my life had changed, allowing me to enjoy these fancier pajamas.

Whether it's about pajamas or life itself, my journey has seen a significant shift. I recall the fall prior to everything falling apart, a subtle whisper that seemed to follow me. It would surface as I cleaned out a closet, saying, "You're doing this to sell the house." Or when I pondered why my relationship felt empty, it softly stated, "You won't be married anymore." I even had glimpses of my future relationship, one that felt different and filled with love.

Whispers are like tiny clues to the path your life is taking. They are subtle hints of the changes you're about to face and the actions you should take. This book started as a whisper—an intuitive nudge that I should begin writing again. It was an inkling that a story was ready to be told and that I was ready to be its storyteller.

Whispers have consistently been an intuitive knowing that everything would fall into place if I persisted. It was the belief that, even though I was navigating a hellish period of life, there would come a time when I could sit on my couch, sip my coffee, listen to the birds singing, and write—just like I'm doing right now.

One of my greatest mentors, Cliffy, imparted a lesson about persistence. Cliffy was a Vietnam War veteran who had been shot in the heart during the war. When he arrived at the hospital, the doctors gave him little chance of survival. His high school sweetheart, the love of his life, heard the news and left him. Lying in the hospital bed, hardly able to move, he made a resolute decision to persist through the pain and use the power of his mind to keep living. Each day, he pushed himself to do a bit more. It began with sitting up, then taking small steps across his room. Eventually, as he continued his rehabilitation, he pushed his body even further. A few years after arriving at the hospital, he walked out, defying the doctors' predictions that he would never walk again.

Cliffy's life epitomized persistence. Every morning, he decided that the day would be amazing, and he would live it to the fullest. His mental fortitude was awe-inspiring. He never allowed his emotions to dictate his life; instead, he observed his emotions and harnessed them to chase his dreams.

Persistence is defined as "a firm or obstinate continuance in a course of action in spite of difficulty or opposition."

During challenging times, one of the most difficult things to do is to keep moving forward despite the obstacles and opposition. It's easy to give up or retreat when life becomes tough. It's simple to make excuses for not taking care of yourself or your well-being.

It was during these times of difficulty that I learned the most about my own strength and determination. It was during those days when life felt overwhelmingly daunting that I realized I could do it, that I could persevere.

Life is full of ups and downs, something every person on this planet knows, and yet it's strange how we seem to forget it when we're in the midst of a downturn.

One thing I discovered that helped me most during those down moments was to be present in the moment, not dwelling too much on the past or anxiously anticipating the future. Fully immersing myself in whatever I was facing allowed me to confront the situation head-on. It provided me with the space to experience the emotions and take the necessary steps to move forward.

In times of stress, I resort to using post-it notes. My friend recently reminded me of this quirk. She said, "Allison, remember how post-it notes were everywhere?"

The lesson in using post-it notes is that there's only so much space on that small piece of paper. You can only write down a few steps. It forces you to focus on the essential tasks.

During that challenging rebuilding phase, I narrowed down the three vital things I needed to survive—literally: a job, a place to live for me and my kids, and a reliable mode of transportation. These three things would provide the stability we required to move forward with our lives. I understand that you may not be in a desperate situation like I found myself in, but if you are, I empathize. The prospect of starting over can be terrifying. Realizing that the life you once knew will never be the same can be a difficult realization, as it was for me. However, once I identified what I truly needed, I knew what I needed to focus on and how I needed to persist each day. I needed to consistently apply for jobs, search for a safe place for my kids and me to live, and find a reliable car to drive. Simple, yet profound.

If you find yourself in a period of transition, I encourage you to ask yourself: What are the things you genuinely need? What are the top three things that will facilitate your transition into the next chapter of your life? Three things might seem overly simplistic, but I learned that the simpler I made it for myself, the better I felt as I accomplished these tasks. These three essentials provided the foundation I needed to rebuild my life.

DAY 4:
EMBRACE THE
"LET'S GO" MINDSET

Today, I want to delve into the importance of adopting a "let's go" attitude. Throughout my healing journey, I've had the incredible support of a friend who has been my rock. When I asked him to describe what he's witnessed me do, he simply said, "let's go."

I refrained from seeking further explanation at the time because I wanted to introspect and understand what this attitude truly means to me. Here's what I've discovered:

A "let's go" attitude means:

Taking action despite your fears: It's about pushing through the paralyzing grip of fear when faced with desperate situations. Even when your brain tells you to stop or freeze, it's important to keep moving forward.

Asking for help: Recognizing that you don't have to navigate life's challenges alone. Seeking assistance from friends and loved ones is not a sign of weakness but a powerful way to overcome adversity.

Seeking adventures to change your perspective: Embracing new experiences and environments to shift your outlook on life. Whether it's traveling to different places, exploring hobbies, or simply stepping out of your comfort zone, adventures can be transformative.

Saying 'yes' to life: Even when life seems to be falling apart, it's crucial to show up for yourself. Saying 'yes' to life means being present, even when it's uncomfortable, and embracing opportunities, no matter how daunting they may seem.

Bringing others with you: Healing doesn't have to be a solitary journey. In fact, it can be more fulfilling when you invite others to share in your adventures and experiences.

In my own healing process, I've found that acknowledging the hard truths and expressing them out loud to trusted friends or family members can release their grip on my mind and heart. This simple act allows me to better care for myself, whether through a nature walk, a soothing bath, or journaling.

Furthermore, the "let's go" attitude extends to seeking help from others. I've learned that it's not only about asking for assistance but also being willing to return the favor and support those in your life.

DAY 5:
THE HEALING JOURNEY
ON A MOUNTAIN HIKE

Appreciate all seasons of life.

One of my favorite activities during my healing journey was hiking a nearby mountain. Each hike brought new insights about myself and my path to recovery.

The first time I tackled this mountain, I was a new mom pushing a stroller with my baby boy. As I ascended, I encountered physical challenges that mirrored my life's struggles. It was a tough climb, but it empowered me to prioritize my own well-being. I realized that I needed to strike a balance between caring for my child and caring for myself.

This realization prompted me to take action. I began to exercise more, even joining intimidating gym classes.

Although it was initially uncomfortable, I gradually built confidence and improved my physical health.

When my life took a turbulent turn, hiking that mountain became my refuge. Those hikes helped me reset my emotions when everything else felt chaotic. They allowed me to savor the beauty of nature and cherish the small moments, like the feeling of the wind on my face.

Throughout the year, I hiked in different seasons, each offering unique lessons. Summer hikes taught me the power of showing up for myself, even in pain. Fall hikes symbolized the transformative shifts in my life, as I embraced a new home, job, and relationships.

Winter hikes were truly magical, mirroring the awe I felt in my life. As my life fell into place, I experienced new relationships and captivating moments. The hikes and my life were in sync, both filled with wonder and awe.

During winter, I also found a shift in my healing journey. I embraced a belief that everything would work out for me and my children. Fear gave way to hope, and I began to anticipate an amazing future.

As the snow melted in spring, my hikes became an opportunity to dream of a new future and process the present. I learned to let go of the past and embrace the power of creation in the now.

In essence, my mountain hikes have taught me to appreciate all seasons of life. Just as seasons change, so does life, and we must embrace these shifts. The pain we experience isn't meant to break us but to reveal our strength and courage. You are not broken; you are whole, unique, and your voice matters. Remember, you matter.

DAY 6:
LET GO

W hat's amusing about this day is that I asked my friend for a concept to write about based on what he's observed in my healing journey. He said "let go," but I initially read it as "let's go." Interestingly, both concepts have played a significant role in my healing process.

To me, "let go" means:

Acknowledging that I am not in control of everything.

Choosing which thoughts about my past I want to retain.

Releasing things and thoughts that no longer serve my best self.

Recognizing the need to let go of certain people or circumstances at times.

My natural inclination is to keep everything in my life as it is because it feels safe and predictable. I'm comfortable with the status quo because I've managed it successfully in the past.

However, life doesn't adhere to our plans; it flows and changes. Life is in a constant state of evolution, and the realities we experience today will not be the same in the future, whether it's a week, a month, or a year from now. Life is characterized by change.

For most of my life, I professed a strong aversion to change. I distinctly remember sitting in a therapist's office once and expressing how much I detested any changes in my life. I wanted everything to remain exactly as it was. The therapist looked at me and reminded me that as long as I was alive, life itself would keep changing. I had a choice: resist it and experience anxiety and fear, or embrace change as an inevitable part of life's journey.

Letting go involves understanding that life will ebb and flow, that change is a constant. We can either resist it and expend energy on anticipating negative outcomes or embrace it, trusting that the universe will guide us to the best possible solutions and allow miracles to unfold.

Letting go also means placing trust in the process. I recall a situation when I was traveling in Paraguay for work. I found myself in the back seat of a car with a group of strangers, asking my translator about our destination. She in turn asked the driver, who seemed unsure. Instead of succumbing to fear and doubt, I chose to let go of my initial anxious thoughts. As I did, I looked out the window and noticed the surroundings were different from what I was accustomed to. We eventually arrived at a travel business office that was safe and beautiful. It was a reminder that I needed to release my fear-driven thoughts and trust the process.

Letting go also involves consciously directing energy toward what we want in life and diverting less energy toward what we don't want. During my healing journey, I began by living day-to-day, but as the fog of confusion cleared, I realized the importance of setting longer-term goals. I decided to plan a short vacation with my kids to Door County. It was a way to create moments of joy and relaxation, and it felt wonderful to shift my focus away from life's worries and toward happiness. Each of us has the power to make this choice.

I've discovered that at different points in life, there are various things we need to let go of. Sometimes it's major aspects like the life we thought we wanted, and sometimes it's smaller things like shifting from a fear-based thought pattern to a more loving one.

Letting go is a powerful healing tool that grants us permission to shed the negative aspects of our lives that hold us back. It allows us to create a new, lighter existence and move freely toward healing and growth.

DAY 7:
BE STILL AND KNOW

M y friend Meghan shared this concept with me over Poke bowls in downtown Madison, WI, before a comedy show. She said, "I believe one of the key concepts in my own healing is to be still and know. I see you, Allison, doing the same thing—trusting that God will guide you to what you need most."

As she spoke, chills ran down my spine, and I knew she was right. Embracing stillness and trusting that I am being guided has been transformative in my healing journey. There were countless days when I lay down to meditate, deliberately inviting stillness into my body. Until that point, meditation was a foreign concept to me, and I couldn't comprehend how ten minutes could shift my energy.

For me, being still often occurred during meditation sessions. Many times, I would lie down on my bed or the floor, placing crystals on my chest while listening to a guided meditation from a stranger named Tamara through my

Calm app. Strangely enough, every time I felt overwhelmed or anxious, the last thing I wanted to do was meditate. My internal dialogue would wrestle with me, urging me to skip the session. The first minute or so of stillness was typically met with racing thoughts, emotions, and shallow breathing. Tamara would guide me to take deep breaths, enabling me to finally connect with my body. I'd start to recenter, feeling a calm stillness wash over me.

Being still during meditation helped me remain present in the moment. In those precious ten minutes, I granted myself permission to just be. I didn't need to be anywhere else or fix anything in my life. The sole objective was to calm my body, to relax into the moment, and to focus on my breath—inhale, exhale.

This practice wasn't something that came naturally to me; I had to cultivate it. Even now, I meditate sporadically, but when I commit to it consistently, I notice a substantial difference in how I engage with life. I feel better, calmer, more capable of handling intense emotions, and more patient with both myself and those around me.

Today, when worry or fear thoughts consume my mind, I excuse myself and meditate. The ensuing lightness and pure peace bring immense joy to my heart.

For those on their healing journey, I strongly recommend considering a meditation practice. Start with just three minutes and gradually work your way up to ten. Pay attention to how you feel before and after each session. If your experience mirrors mine, you'll notice a dramatic shift in your well-being.

The second part of this concept is "to know." This year, my chosen word is "trust." I believe that "to know" and "trust" are intricately linked. You need trust to truly know, and you need to know in order to trust. Both aspects are vital in your healing journey, as well as in trusting that a higher power is guiding your life.

I have a sticker that reads, "God is always conspiring for my highest good." I love it because it reminds me that even during challenging times, everything is ultimately working out in my favor. Every problem or difficulty I face is leading me toward something more wonderful. I'm being prepared to lead a life filled with favor and grace, guided along a path uniquely designed for me.

For most of my life, I attempted to control every aspect of it. I wanted to manipulate circumstances and outcomes, believing that by sheer force of will, I could make things happen. However, when my life crumbled and I lost my "dream" home, "perfect" relationship, and other aspects of what I thought was my "perfect" life, I was forced to confront the fact that I am not in control.

This realization hit me hard. I could certainly exert effort and energy toward my goals, but ultimately, I was being led in a direction only a higher power understood fully.

A year and a half after all that upheaval, I find myself grateful for the challenges that brought me to this point in my life. I experience more love, peace, and joy than I ever thought possible. My priorities have shifted, and I've gained a new perspective on what truly matters in life. Even the people I now hold close and dear, some of the most loving individuals, were complete strangers to me just a year ago. It's astonishing.

Consider today that you are embarking on a beautiful adventure called life. As you surrender your preconceived notions and plans, you will attract more of the things you desire. By finding stillness within yourself, you will experience peace like never before. As you come to know and trust that everything is unfolding in your favor, you'll relinquish the need for control.

Some of the most profound lessons I've learned in my hardest moments have led me to a life far beyond what I once imagined—a life characterized by love, deep connections, relationships, and happiness.

My wish for you is to take a moment to recognize your own power in being still and knowing.

DAY 7.5:
HEALING WHEN IT HURTS

What about the days when brokenness doesn't feel beautiful? Those days when a cloud of sadness hovers, and you can't escape feelings of inadequacy, unworthiness, and not measuring up.

What do you do then?

As I write this, tears are welling up in my eyes. Today was one of those days when everything just felt really tough.

Eighteen years ago, on this very day, I was wearing a white dress, walking down an aisle, laughing, and feeling incredibly happy. I was filled with hope, excited about the new life I was starting.

Today, I sat at my son's lacrosse game, watching my ex-husband and his new girlfriend play the role of a family with my kids. My heart ached. Witnessing it sucked the breath out of me.

Don't get me wrong—I don't want to be married to him anymore, and I don't regret my decisions. I suppose I just felt a deep sadness—a sadness that my hopes and dreams for that life never materialized.

Have you ever seen a glass plate shatter into a million pieces when it hits the floor? That's what happened to my life. It shattered into countless fragments, scattered, with some pieces lost forever.

Throughout the day, I tried everything to distract myself from the pain, to stay busy and avoid facing the brokenness that I felt—the sadness that loomed over me, the shattered pieces that would never fit back together.

I know you might be waiting for some profound solution to this pain. You might be expecting a grand revelation that will help you when despair creeps in during your own healing journey.

But it's not profound.

I took a shower, put on my pajamas, ate some egg rolls, and started typing this. I took small steps to care for myself a bit more. I acknowledged that I was feeling sad. There was no one here to comfort me, so I had to do something to ease my heartache and make myself feel a bit better. These small actions help—the little things I do to nurture myself when I'm sad. Making myself feel special, sipping some tea, reading a book, laughing at a show, going for a hike, or calling a friend.

During my journey, I've learned that it's crucial to honor my emotions and let them surface. Wishing them away doesn't work. Ignoring them only makes them resurface later, often stronger. I simply allow myself to feel, to cry, and to acknowledge that it's okay to hurt and heal. It's okay to be human. My life is incredibly wonderful, filled with amazing blessings and opportunities. Still, I need to take the time to experience my emotions fully.

Taking time to feel is a concept I never embraced before my life shattered. I suppressed my feelings, denied myself the release of tears, and pretended everything was fine when it wasn't. For years, I buried my hurt and pain, avoiding any discussion of it. I thought that by pretending I was okay, I would eventually be fine.

I discovered that pretending wasn't the solution. Denying my truth wasn't healthy. Ignoring the signs that my life was about to shatter into a million pieces was a misguided way to live.

So, here I am, sitting with my sadness. Mourning the "perfect" life that never was and realizing that it was never truly mine or even the truth. It wasn't my truth.

Amid the brokenness, I discovered my real truth—being deeply in love with God, myself, my children, my family, and the incredible people in my life. My truth is believing in the goodness that life has in store for me, having faith that everything will work out better than I could have imagined. I possess a profound inner knowing that I can pick up the shards of glass and gradually mend my plate, infusing it with gold and wisdom. Some pieces may be lost, but they were the wrong pieces for the mosaic of my life. I let them go and embraced the pieces that truly mattered—my faith, family, friends, health, work, passions, creativity, joy, and peace. These were the building blocks for a new, beautiful life.

On your own healing journey, you might yearn to pick up all the broken pieces and reassemble them just as they were before. You might long for the way your life used to be, wishing to go back. But what I've learned is that life flows continuously. It changes and evolves, and to navigate it, we must allow things to unfold as they were meant to. Everything that happens, whether good, terrible, difficult, or great, serves a purpose. You might not understand that purpose right now, but one day, you'll look back at this broken time in your life and realize how it all makes perfect sense.

You will emerge as a more authentic version of yourself, liberated from conditioning. Now, you are building something even more beautiful—broken and beautiful.

DAY 8:
EMBRACING LIMITLESSNESS

U pon awakening, I found myself filled with a lighter spirit. Last night, before slipping into slumber, I engaged in a powerful activity—one that I wholeheartedly encourage you to undertake during your healing journey.

First, I journaled. This practice has been my faithful companion throughout my entire healing journey. Daily, I pour my feelings, thoughts, gratitude, struggles— everything—onto those pages. This process helps me unravel the chaos surrounding me, providing clarity amid the confusion.

Last night, however, I embarked on something deeper. I delved into the origins of my self-doubt. I confronted the negative stories I'd been telling myself. These insidious narratives had been holding me back, preventing me from fully stepping into my future. They acted as anchors, weighing down my heart and constraining me to a smaller existence.

As I transcribed some of these toxic beliefs and words onto the pages of my journal, I was taken aback. If someone in my life spoke to me in that same disparaging manner, I would promptly sever ties with them. Yet, day in and day out, I was walking around subjecting myself to this internal self-talk.

How you speak to yourself matters profoundly on your healing journey. The thoughts you cultivate and the way you converse with yourself internally have the power to reshape your brain. Acknowledging this, ensure that your thoughts serve the best version of yourself by being consistently positive.

If you currently find yourself trapped in a relentless cycle of negative self-talk, unable to discern any glimmer of positivity, seek help from someone you trust. Open up to them about your struggles and ask for a few positive aspects about yourself that you can focus on. Then, truly listen to their perspective.

The lightness that will grace your heart and mind after this process is genuinely transformative. Recognizing how these subconscious beliefs have been silently influencing your behavior day in and day out can be liberating. Your mind should gradually feel less chaotic.

Allow me to share a brief anecdote concerning negative beliefs. Once, I attended an international conference with participants from over 100 countries. We engaged in an exercise similar to the one I've described, where we documented our self-doubts and negative thoughts. Initially, I assumed that due to our diverse backgrounds and life experiences, we would each interpret this activity differently. I couldn't have been more wrong.

Every individual in that room, regardless of their origins, experienced self-doubt. Each one grappled with negative beliefs about themselves. Irrespective of their positions or wealth, they all shared in this common human experience.

Recognizing this truth was incredibly liberating. I wasn't alone. Surrounded by people from all walks of life, I discovered that we all harbored beliefs that did not serve our best interests.

You are not alone in your self-doubt. Every person on this planet has grappled with self-doubt at some point in their lives. The distinction lies in how we choose to deal with these beliefs. If we continue to embrace them, they will proliferate and sow turmoil and pain in our lives. However, if we identify them and release their grip on us, we can move forward with hope and lightness.

One of the most remarkable aspects of my healing journey is the realization that each of us possesses the opportunity to transform into a truer version of ourselves. It's akin to cleaning out the cluttered closet of our minds. Some thoughts and beliefs no longer serve us; they once held us back. As we release them, we move forward infused with new energy and enthusiasm for life. Don't be afraid to methodically edit the closet of your mind. Extract those negative narratives, discard them, and bar them from reentry. They may have served the older version of yourself, but they no longer align with the new version you are becoming.

Throughout your healing journey, you'll notice yourself evolving into a more authentic self. Your responses to life's challenges will shift, and you will likely extend more grace, both to yourself and to others. In my own healing odyssey, I found laughter becoming a more frequent visitor in my life. I laugh a lot now, reveling in the sheer joy of it. Seeking reasons to laugh in life has become a delightful quest.

Grant yourself permission to seek out moments of joy, even if they are seemingly small. A single moment of laughter can set the wheels of transformation in motion in your life. Remember that you are in the process of repairing the broken pieces in your life and forging something new and special. This process isn't easy, but it is profoundly worthwhile. Through the intentionality you apply to rebuild and heal, you craft a fresh script for your life. This new script dictates how you will show up in your new life—a life brimming with happiness, love, and peace. This new life will feel distinctly different from any other time in your existence, and that difference is a beautiful one. You are creating a new way of being in the world. Your past self was never wrong, but now, through growth, you can show up in a lighter, more expansive manner.

Take a moment to honor your newfound lightness. Extend gratitude to yourself for embarking on this universal mission of becoming a truer version of yourself.

You are precisely who the world needs—the most authentic and genuine rendition of you.

DAY 9:
NO LIMITS

*My devotional today said, "With God,
all things are possible."*

Maintaining a limitless mindset can be challenging amidst trials. Believing that you'll be okay and everything will work out may feel uncomfortable. How can you navigate pain while contemplating greatness? It may not seem logical, but that's precisely what's required.

"Limitless" means without end, limit, or boundary. When I ponder that definition, I envision a limitless person as someone who anticipates tomorrow will surpass today. One of my friends holds a positive expectation that things will effortlessly fall into place for him, and they usually do—often better than he anticipates. He's conditioned his mind to consistently harbor this outlook, enabling him to remain receptive to amazing occurrences, even when least expected. Perhaps he's hiking and suddenly encounters a breathtaking vista, or embarks on a trip that exceeds all expectations. Because he assumes that things will align, they often do. This is the essence of a limitless mindset—believing unconditionally that life will unfold as it should.

However, if you've recently endured hardships, you might still find yourself in survival mode—a state where your instinct is to retract into yourself for protection. Embracing limitations may provide a sense of comfort and peace during the healing process, and that's perfectly acceptable. I too retreated into myself during my healing journey. I restricted social interactions, focused on nurturing my children and myself, and sought solace in activities like long walks, hot baths, and journaling.

In the midst of pain, it's natural to feel apprehensive about dreaming big and impose limits on your potential. And let me be candid: I'm perfectly okay admitting it. I was in the midst of healing from significant trauma and needed the time and space to mend my shattered self. I needed to afford myself and my children the opportunity to heal, to feel safe, loved, and protected.

So, how can you maintain a limitless mindset while traversing the path of healing?

During my own healing journey, I discovered that focusing on one or two achievable goals and wholeheartedly believing in their attainment embodies a limitless mindset. By fixating on these goals, you can envision a brighter future and foster hope and tranquility. The chosen goal should invigorate and inspire you, serving as a beacon of optimism amidst the turmoil.

Around four months into my healing journey, I had laid the groundwork for transitioning into single parenthood— securing housing, employment, and transportation. With these essentials in place, I shifted my focus to setting goals for the future. One of my initial aspirations was to treat my children to a vacation at our favorite destination. In August, we embarked on this adventure, reveling in the simple joy of floating on the ocean waves. It was truly magical!

Experiencing the fulfillment of a limitless goal underscored how much energy I had expended dwelling on past pain, while neglecting my dreams and aspirations. I yearned to embrace a life of possibility and joy, liberated from the shackles of negativity. This epiphany struck me one day as I perused my journal entries, noticing a pattern of complaints and grievances. That day, I resolved to cultivate gratitude by documenting the little blessings in my life. Initially challenging, this practice gradually revealed countless reasons for gratitude—whether it was the serenity of a forest hike, the infectious laughter of my children, or the warmth of friendship.

Over time, I began to perceive limitless possibilities everywhere, embracing the notion that even amidst adversity, life can yield beautiful outcomes. Every experience, whether pleasant or painful, contributes to the grand tapestry of our lives. It's about acknowledging and embracing each chapter, recognizing that even the darkest moments pave the way for enlightenment and growth. Embrace it. Own it.

DAY 10:
MIRACLES

*"There are only two ways to live
your life. One is as though nothing
is a miracle. The other is as though
everything is a miracle."*

—*Albert Einstein*

M iracles abound, even in life's darkest moments. The key lies in attuning yourself to their presence and recognizing their role in guiding you forward.

Embracing a miracle mindset entails viewing your thoughts and experiences through a lens of love. Recently, I found myself immersed in a difficult conversation with a friend—a conversation that tugged at my heartstrings and stirred deep emotions. In the past, I might have recoiled from such vulnerability, opting to sever ties rather than confront discomfort. Yet, amidst this exchange, I experienced a shift—a miracle, if you will. It enabled me to extend compassion to my friend, to listen without judgment, and to acknowledge their perspective with an open heart. That, to me, epitomizes the essence of a miracle mindset.

By reshaping your perceptions of life's trials and tribulations, you can alter the very fabric of your existence. Choosing love over fear empowers you to extend grace to yourself during moments of self-doubt, fostering a sense of inner peace. Conversely, succumbing to fearful thoughts only exacerbates our suffering. While this loving mindset may not yield immediate results, cultivating a habit of seeking the silver lining in every situation invites miracles into our lives.

These miracles, or "pinch me" moments, serve as poignant reminders of life's inherent beauty. Whether it's basking in the splendor of nature, forging deep connections with others, or witnessing the universe align in our favor, these moments leave us awestruck. As we attune ourselves to the frequency of miracles, we become attuned to the guiding hand of destiny. What's meant for us will invariably find its way into our lives, while that which isn't will gracefully depart.

DAY 11:
SHOW ME

As I relinquished control and surrendered to the natural flow of life, remarkable transformations began to unfold before my eyes.

As I began to trust that everything was unfolding exactly as it should and that I needed to relinquish control and allow life to unfold, remarkable things started happening to me.

The first step I took was to ask for help. In the past, when faced with difficulties, I used to shut down and keep everything to myself. I would hide away, shed tears, and put on a facade of normalcy. However, I soon realized that navigating life solo was an arduous task. Withholding my true feelings from others was not conducive to my well-being. I required the support and prayers of my family and friends, particularly during challenging times.

Recently, I encountered a particularly tough day where everything seemed to unravel, leaving me overwhelmed with sadness. My initial instinct was to withdraw into myself, to suffer in silence and handle my pain alone. But then, I remembered a new approach I had been trying: when faced with adversity, I would consider the opposite of my usual response and act accordingly. So, on this occasion, I summoned the courage to confide in two dear friends about what was happening. I reached out to them, asking for their prayers and support. Throughout the day, they checked in on me, offering words of comfort and reassurance. Their unwavering presence reminded me that I was not alone in my struggles.

During the healing process, it's crucial to seek assistance when needed.

Another strategy I employed was to ask the universe to "show me" the right path. I would request clear signs indicating what my next steps should be in life. For instance, when deliberating between job opportunities, I sought guidance from a friend who had spent his entire career in the corporate world. He provided valuable insights that influenced my decision to choose the privately held company over the corporate position. This advice came shortly after I had asked for clear direction, underscoring the significance of paying attention to messages conveyed through significant conversations.

If you find yourself curious about something, asking the universe to "show me" may lead you to the answers you seek.

There is peace in knowing that you are always being guided. You are continually progressing in your journey. The things meant for you will inevitably find their way into your life.

DAY 12: ALONE

As my life was crumbling, the word "alone" became my greatest fear. Being alone felt like a failure to create the beautiful life I desired. It seemed like a personal failure, as if I wasn't enough to make it work. Even today, this fear still creeps into my life. I grapple with thoughts that I might be alone forever.

But I recognize these thoughts as false. I am never truly alone. God is always with me. I have my children, who will always be a part of my life. My family and some of the most amazing friends surround me, providing unwavering support.

Last night, I found myself grappling with tough relationship issues. I felt rejected, sad, and upset. Despite holding onto a sliver of hope for the relationship to work, the pain in my heart was overwhelming. I cried at work, on my way to work, and had to hide our picture on my desk. I knew a conversation was looming, one that might spell the end of what we had. I avoided it, driven by the fear of being alone and losing his love.

There's something special about having someone to share your life with. Someone you can confide in, who supports you through struggles and celebrates your victories.

But when that support and love dissipate, your heart aches, and you feel alone. You feel a sense of despair, clinging to any hope of salvaging the relationship, even when all signs point to letting go.

Letting go is difficult. Leaving behind dreams for a relationship that no longer serves either of you is hard work. Recognizing that your pain outweighs the happiness you once shared is a harsh reality.

Last night, I poured my heart out to one of my closest friends while indulging in a strawberry sundae on my patio. I shared everything I had been experiencing in the relationship. She asked a simple question: "Allison, is this relationship easy for you?" My answer was a resounding "No." It had been difficult for a long time. If I'm honest, it had been difficult from the start. I blamed my healing journey for the strain in our relationship, feeling broken and unworthy of his love.

Yet, here I am, still holding on.

What does the future hold for our relationship? I honestly have no clue. I've given myself permission to let it go. If it's meant to return, it will. If not, perhaps it was never meant to be.

So here I am, facing the prospect of being alone once more. Alone to confront life's challenges. Alone. It makes me sad and angry not to have a partner. I yearn for love and support, to create a beautiful family filled with love and happiness.

I don't want to be alone.

My strategy for coping with this feeling is to schedule activities with friends or family on the days or weekends I would be alone. Instead of dwelling at home, I push myself to go out, even when I don't feel like it.

The feeling of loneliness will eventually fade, replaced by the knowledge that I am still whole and happy, even without the relationship. I recognize that I likely knew for some time that I needed to walk away. I had outgrown what the relationship could offer.

Letting go is hard, one of the hardest things you can do. But living a lie, clinging to something that no longer serves you, is even harder.

If you find yourself trying endlessly to salvage a relationship that's not working, maybe it's time to let go. Release it to the universe, asking for guidance and love.

As you release it, send it love, happy memories, and all the goodness you can muster.

Then, give yourself space to breathe.

Allow yourself to feel the feelings you've been denying. Let the pain and hurt bubble to the surface. Cry, yell into your pillow, let it all out.

In my healing journey, releasing the pain and hurt has been one of the most therapeutic experiences. Allowing myself permission to feel my emotions, to be vulnerable, has been healing, albeit uncomfortable.

You don't have to walk this journey alone. Ask for help. Share your pain with someone you trust. By sharing your darkness, you'll find you're no longer alone in the dark. You can both live in the light.

Today, choose to live in the light.

DAY 13:
SHIFTS

A t this stage in your healing journey, you might notice some significant shifts taking place. These shifts are a result of your growth and healing.

For me, these shifts began when I consciously started seeking things to be grateful for in my life. It started with simple gratitude lists as I sat on my couch, morning prayers in hand. I found myself grateful for the little things – a cup of coffee, the comfort of my couch, the peace that surrounded me, and the beauty in my surroundings.

Gradually, these lists grew longer. My heart shifted from focusing on the negative to embracing the positive.

As I began to seek the good, more good started flowing into my life. It was like a magical power I had never tapped into before.

Remember, when you look for the good, you'll find more of it.

DAY 14:
BE THE ONE FOR SOMEONE

This day's reflection is inspired by a mother who is watching over us from above. She left behind a legacy for those who remember her – to be the one for someone.

During my own healing journey, I initially focused solely on my own pain. I was engulfed in deep anguish, fearing the unknown. I needed to prioritize my own needs and those of my children, something I hadn't fully recognized before. I had spent most of my life trying to make others happy, being the self-proclaimed "fixer" who excelled at helping others while often neglecting my own needs.

Then tragedy struck, and I had to channel all my energy into crafting a new life for myself and my children – a life built on stability, safety, love, and peace. I had no other choice; no one else could do it for me. I had to make it work, to focus, to want it, to pray for it, and to do everything in my power to secure the life we deserved after enduring so much pain.

And that's precisely what I did. I spent months prioritizing our most basic needs for survival. At its core, we needed stability – a job for me, a safe home, and a reliable car. These simple things, though often taken for granted, felt like the most incredible gifts. If you've ever been in that place as a single mother, struggling to provide for your children, you understand the determination to make it work, to fight for a dream that sometimes seems impossible.

One by one, these essentials fell into place – first the house, then the car, and finally the job. Each blessing brought a new sense of peace and healing. We were going to be okay; we were rebuilding our lives, creating something beautiful.

But even as stability and peace returned to my life, I sensed something missing. I still wanted to give, even though it seemed I had nothing left to give. Or so I thought.

What can one do to uplift others, I wondered? All I had at that moment was my encouragement. I began looking for people in my life who needed support, and I made it a point to be the one for them. Often, it was my children. I would look into their eyes, kiss their foreheads, and reassure them of their safety and the unwavering love surrounding us. I'd remind them that we would make it through, and they knew their mom would never, ever, ever give up. I can't express how many times I repeated those words during our journey.

In your own journey, whether in times of joy or sorrow, remember to never, ever, ever give up. Brighter days lie ahead. New people will come into your life, bearing blessings you couldn't foresee. There is much to look forward to, even during the darkest days. The light is coming; blessings are on their way.

My Grandma Char used to say, "With every trial or hardship you face in life, you'll have a blessing of equal or greater magnitude."

Imagine all the wonderful things you'll experience after enduring pain. The life you'll lead will surpass your wildest imagination. Love will penetrate deeper, connections with family and friends will strengthen, you'll feel valued in your work, strong in your health, and at peace with yourself. Your heart will heal, and that healing will unveil a new version of yourself – one capable of enduring much, yet feeling more at peace than ever before.

I discovered that by losing everything I deemed important in my life – my "dream" house, my "perfect" marriage, and everything that accompanied them – I was not crushed, as I had feared. Instead, on the other side of that pain, I found a profound revelation. My "dream" house did not equate to happiness; it only caused stress as I attempted to fit into a life that didn't align with my true desires. My "perfect" marriage was far from perfect; it had been broken all along. Leaving it allowed me to honor my needs and care for myself in new ways, ultimately finding a level of peace that had eluded me for so long.

Letting go is demanding work. In the midst of the messy middle of letting go, everything feels uncomfortable. I questioned everything constantly, struggling to control a situation beyond my control. I had to make peace with the fact that, no matter my efforts, I needed to trust the unfolding of my life, even the painful parts. I had to stop forcing it and let it flow through me.

Flowing with life means allowing things to happen. Of course, there are battles worth fighting for. But some things that initially make no sense may turn out to be extraordinary blessings. The very things you cling to might be the very things you look back on, realizing you should have let go of them long ago.

Whom could you support in your life today? Even in your own pain, you have the capacity to share love and encouragement with someone else. Is it your children? Consider how you can show them just how special they are. A small note or a small gift can make them feel valued and loved. Perhaps there's a friend who would appreciate a phone call; reach out, engage in a conversation, and listen to what they're experiencing in life. Offer support and love. If there's an elderly person living alone, pay them a visit. Bring some donuts, ask them to share their life stories, share some of your own, and share a good laugh.

When you reach a point in life where you can intentionally be there for others, you'll discover what truly matters and what doesn't. You'll feel your heart swell with love from the wonderful people around you. Every conversation, positive interaction, unexpected hug, or hike up a mountain will be a gift. You'll seek out ways to help those in your life realize how amazing they are, going out of your way to remind them.

In this process, you'll understand what's genuinely important and what isn't. You'll feel your heart expand with love from the incredible people surrounding you. Every conversation, positive interaction, random hug, or mountain hike will be a gift. You'll actively seek ways to help the people in your life realize their incredible worth, going the extra mile to remind them. In the process, you'll tap into your own power, recognizing your strength and resilience. Even after enduring immense pain, you'll have grown into an even more remarkable version of yourself – one filled with compassion, love, goodness, and hope. You'll strive to build a new, beautiful life, and you'll intentionally surround yourself with people and resources to make that vision a reality.

Trust this process. Trust yourself. Trust that you are continuously being guided. Trust that everything will work out better than you could have imagined. Someday, when you look back on the pain you've endured, you'll realize that, even though it hurt, it was one of the greatest blessings. Without it, you wouldn't have crafted the life you now lead – a life overflowing with love, joy, happiness, peace, and profound meaning. You wouldn't have become this new version of yourself. Embrace your beautifully broken self, own it, and understand that this beautifully broken version is precisely what the world needs – it needs you!

DAY 15:
YOU ARE WILDLY CAPABLE

"Never forget how wildly capable you
are."

—Allison Michels

There are times in life when it seems like everything is going wrong, and in those moments, we tend to forget just how capable we truly are. We lose sight of our strength and power as we become preoccupied with the challenges life throws at us.

Today, I woke up with a specific intention – to fill my day with positivity and gratitude. I made a conscious choice to focus on all the wonderful things happening in my life and to channel my energy into manifesting even more greatness. I began by jotting down a list of people and things I'm thankful for. I delved into my devotionals and practiced meditation. These seemingly small actions set the tone for my day and put me in a positive mindset.

The choices and thoughts we have upon waking can significantly impact the rest of our day. If you can carve out 30 minutes of solitude before others in your life awaken, I encourage you to do so. Sip your coffee, get comfortable, and set your intentions for the day. Use this time to craft the kind of day you desire, rather than starting off reactively and stressed.

In my own growth journey, waking up early has been a game-changer. I prioritize my sleep, so there are days when I allow myself extra rest. However, for the most part, I wake up early to have this time alone, to pray, reflect, and ease into the day.

This practice has had a profound impact on how I navigate the rest of my day. Even on difficult days, this time feels sacred as it allows me to process my emotions in a safe space and within a set timeframe. Once this period ends, I leave those thoughts and feelings behind on my couch and face the challenges of the day with renewed determination.

I am wildly capable. I can do this. I'll figure it out. All the people and resources I need are aligning to support my best outcome.

These are the affirmations I often repeat to myself to remind me of my strength. When confronting unknown situations with uncertain outcomes, I've learned to create the desired outcome in my mind. I focus my energy on envisioning everything working out better than I could have anticipated. This positive mindset has consistently yielded favorable results. While fear-based thoughts may creep in during stressful times, I allow myself to acknowledge them and then invest every ounce of energy into ensuring that things work out positively.

This approach has been like a magic wand in my healing journey. Intentionally seeking the desired outcome, relinquishing the need to know "how" it will happen, and simply trusting the process have helped me immensely. The "how" always falls into place, and I navigate it with curiosity, eager to see how it unfolds.

DAY 16:
EMBRACING THE REORDERING

"The universe is always reordering
your life for the better. Don't fight it."

—Allison Michels

Have you ever found yourself amidst a whirlwind of
sudden changes? Perhaps you relocated, landed a
new job, faced a health scare, tied the knot, or underwent a
divorce. Change, in its myriad forms, can sweep through our
lives unexpectedly.

In the past year, my life underwent a complete overhaul. My
home, marital status, vehicle, job, even my last name—all
changed. Initially, I clung desperately to familiarity amidst
the upheaval. My marriage ended, yet I held onto a flicker
of hope. The home I cherished was sold, now replaced with
gratitude for its absence. My sleek car was replaced with one
more fuel-efficient, a pleasant surprise. Transitioning from
owning a business to a more stable job brought unforeseen

security. Even my last name changed, a transition that felt surprisingly natural.

Sometimes, the universe recognizes the need for change and orchestrates it, rearranging every aspect of our lives. For too long, I resisted change, fearing its uncertainties. However, this past year of transformation taught me invaluable lessons:

1. **Initial Confusion:** At first, change may seem bewildering, devoid of logic. Yet, with time, clarity emerges. Looking back, I now see the purpose behind each change, even the most challenging ones. Every experience, even the toughest, holds a lesson.

2. **Embracing Difficulty:** Change is inherently tough, disrupting the comfort of routine. Transitioning from predictability to uncertainty requires resilience. Yet, amidst the turmoil, lies the potential for profound growth. It's crucial to be gentle with oneself, allowing space for reflection and adaptation.

3. **Reevaluation:** Amidst change, we're prompted to reassess our priorities. In the chaos, I yearned for peace, love, and simplicity. Stripping away the clutter, I focused on what truly mattered: family, health, and personal growth. Through prayer and introspection, I found solace amidst the upheaval.

4. **Accepting Flux:** Life is a constant ebb and flow of change. Resisting it only leads to stagnation. Embracing change, however daunting, opens doors to new opportunities and perspectives.

5. **Trusting the Journey:** Trusting the process of change is an ongoing lesson. It requires patience and faith, especially during tumultuous times. Though understanding may elude us, trusting that every twist and turn serves a purpose enables growth and transformation.

Despite its challenges, change is an inevitable part of life. Resisting it only prolongs the discomfort. Instead, embracing change offers a path to self-discovery and fulfillment. Each upheaval, though daunting, propels us toward a richer, more authentic existence—a life we're meant to embrace fully.

DAY 17:
I HEARD YOUR PRAYER.
TRUST MY TIMING.
— GOD

My word for the year is trust. Trusting myself, trusting others, and trusting God after enduring so much pain has undoubtedly been one of the toughest aspects of my journey.

When life throws you a curveball, you can catch it and move forward. But when it feels like the curveballs keep coming from all directions, leaving bruises all over your body from the pain—it's a whole new level.

What do you do when you find yourself in a place of confusion, hurt, and pain, not knowing what step to take next?

Pray.

Seriously. That's the only thing you can do. When you're devoid of answers and everything seems beyond your control, you need to pray for guidance. Even the smallest nudge in a direction can help you move forward in life.

I've always had faith, but it wasn't until my life spiraled out of control that I began to pray dangerous prayers. Hard prayers. Real prayers. Prayers of truth and wisdom. These are the prayers where you ask God to be brutally honest with you, guiding you in the best direction, even if it seems contrary to where you want to go.

Then comes the hardest part: trusting those answers and following their lead.

Trust.

Trusting can be the most challenging part of healing. Trusting that the pain will heal. Trusting that one day, laughter will return. Trusting that one day, you'll find true love. Trusting that one day, you'll experience pure joy.

After praying those difficult prayers for clarity in my life, I found myself wanting to retract them. I'd pray, "Hey God, help me with this…" Then, the next day, I'd wake up trying to figure out how to control the situation.

Don't do that.

Pray to God and surrender the problem to Him fully and completely. Stop dwelling on it if you can. Let it go. And trust that it's being worked out. Trust that God has a plan for the perfect outcome.

One thing I remind myself after being in a low and praying for help is that God is always working for my highest good. Always!

If that's the case, why worry? If doubts and worries plague me, I'll grab my journal and list all the ways God has blessed me and my children. I might even review some old prayers to see if they've been answered.

And without fail, they always are! Every. Single. Time!

What I've learned from praying is that I need to trust the answer God gives me. Even if it's not what I want to hear at the time, I know that eventually, it will make perfect sense.

Another aspect of the praying process is God's timing. I've discovered that if God truly wants something to happen in my life, it will happen swiftly. Things will align. Everything I need and desire will manifest, even better than I imagined.

What if the things I worry about actually work in my favor? What if the things that stress me out resolve themselves, and I realize there was no need for all that stress? What if I trusted that everything I need—love, job, health, friends, money—was aligning to come into my life?

If I trusted God's timing and focused all my energy on things working out, what would I have to worry about? Would I feel stressed? Alone? Worried? Probably not, because it's not mine to hold onto anymore.

One of my friends tries to control everything in his life. When he reaches a point where he can't figure it out, he gives up or pushes it away. As he was doing this once, he asked me why I don't do the same. I told him that if I give it to God and trust that it'll work out in His timing, it typically does, and even better than I could have imagined. I've witnessed it time and time again.

That's not to say it isn't hard work or painful in the process. If you're in love and the person you love expresses doubts, your heart may physically ache. You might feel bewildered, angry, and sorrowful. But if you pray for wisdom, asking God to either keep that person in your life if they're meant to be there or remove them if they're not, then trust in the outcome, you'll feel a newfound freedom. Perhaps this prayer will lead to a conversation strengthening your relationship. Maybe you both needed this pause to heal old wounds and come together stronger. Or perhaps that person wasn't meant to be a loving partner, and staying together would only bring more pain.

God always has a plan. Trust it and trust His timing.

DAY 18:
YOU ARE WORTHY!

I n the depths of despair remembering your worthiness can be difficult. In those low points in my own life I found myself focused on everything I wasn't.

So, how can you possibly go from a place of not believing in your worthiness to owning it?

Today it meant having a friend text me a reminder that said: Sending love your way!! You are beautiful, strong, and so worthy of great love and partnership. You are so incredibly loved! Do not let anyone make you feel otherwise. I understand how that can feel, but logically, you know how amazing you are.

Sometimes in your despair you need the people in your life to send you special reminders. You need to turn off the negative thoughts or internal voices trying to convince you of anything other than your awesomeness.

You are awesome!

On hard days I would ask my best friends for reminders. It felt weird at first, but I would do the same thing for them, so I felt like it was okay.

The important thing I needed to remember is that my worthiness did not depend on anyone else's thoughts about me. My worthiness is not dependent on receiving love in a relationship. It's not depended on my job, my car, my bank account. My worthiness is not dependent on what happened to me in the past or even what I look like.

My worthiness is based on God's love for me and my love for myself. That's it!

No one can or should be able to take your worthiness of all of the goodness life has to offer away from you. Your worth is not dependent on them at all. Even if they are trying to convince you that it is, it isn't! You are worthy despite their feelings toward you. You are loved and special for being you.

During relationship issues or challenges in life it might be easy to believe the negative thoughts that you did something to deserve the hurt. You may wonder if you could have changed it. You may wonder if you are actually enough to get through the storms life is throwing at you...you are.

DAY 19:
WHAT GOD SENDS YOU
WILL ARRIVE IN CLARITY,
NOT CONFUSION

H ave you ever faced a change in your life where you had two options? One option appears superior on paper, and you try to convince yourself it's the better choice. It promises a "simple" and "easy" life.

I believe too many people in the world opt for the easy path in life. They gravitate toward what they perceive as familiar.

The other choice isn't as straightforward; it requires effort, but deep down, you know it will lead to a more fulfilling life than anything you've experienced before. You'll feel more love, more fulfillment, and more contentment.

Clarity arises from knowing and trusting yourself. The problem arises when we trust the fearful thoughts in our heads, attempting to "protect" us from what we know in our hearts is the right next step in our lives. It feels uncomfortable to care so deeply about the outcome. Yet, caring about the result is also a sign. Something or someone in your life that occupies your thoughts and stirs your emotions is clarity.

During my life transitions, I found it beneficial to listen to my heart and move in the direction it urges. Initially, confusion may persist because I've been mired in overthinking about potential outcomes or what I desire. The only true way to know is to maintain hope that the choice will turn out better than I could have imagined.

When I find myself mired in confusion or indecision, with thoughts swirling in my head, I pause, grab a piece of paper, and jot down all the questions plaguing me. They may be negative queries like: what if I get hurt? What if it doesn't work? What if it's painful?

Then, I take those same questions and flip them to their opposites. What if I feel loved? What if it works out beyond my wildest dreams? What if it's amazing?

I've discovered that the mind will readily conjure up countless reasons why something won't work if you let it. The true challenge lies in training it to search for all the reasons why it could work and will work. Your brain is wired to protect you and will instinctively generate myriad reasons why you should shy away from anything good in your life.

But what if it works out beyond my wildest dreams, and I simply let it?

Don't allow fear to dictate crucial decisions in your life. Fearful thoughts breed confusion.

Instead, let loving thoughts take the reins. Loving thoughts are the ones that cultivate beauty in our lives. Focusing on kindness and love will revolutionize every aspect of your life. Thinking lovingly about yourself will elevate your self-esteem and extend grace to others. Treating the people in your life with love and kindness will make them feel seen and understood. Many people rarely experience such genuine care, so if you can demonstrate your care through actions, you'll be amazed by the depth of connection you'll feel with others. Embracing a mindset of loving kindness will elevate you to a higher vibrational frequency. You'll experience a lightness and a sense of guidance.

I recently went out for dinner to have what I anticipated to be a difficult conversation. Before stepping in, I prayed for peace, love, and kindness to envelop us. As the person I was meeting arrived, my heart swelled with a loving sense of peace. When we began our conversation, I expressed my desire for us to approach it with love and kindness. We each shared our feelings in a compassionate manner, holding hands and gazing into each other's eyes. We exchanged affectionate gestures, and it turned out to be one of the most beautiful conversations I've ever had because we both approached it with such positive intentions.

Clarity emerges from sharing love and kindness with others.

Confusion arises from sharing fears and pain with others.

Clarity arises when you give yourself space to think and time to process emotions.

Confusion arises from sharing in the heat of the moment, when emotions run high.

Granting yourself time and grace can completely alter the outcome of a situation. Being deliberate about creating room for miracles to manifest is also beneficial.

I always believe that the most remarkable things are about to unfold in my life. I search for signs of impending miracles swirling around me.

Miracles are always on their way—expect them!

Each and everything that happens in your life is for a reason. The challenges teach you lessons. The great times teach you appreciation and love. All along your life journey everything that happens is for a reason.

You may not know what the reason is at first, but eventually the reason will become apparent. At first it may feel like you were stripped of love or a life you always wanted, but in time the truth will emerge, and you will understand why that had to happen in your life.

Today, trust your worthiness. Know that you are worthy of all the good. You are enough and things will always work out in your favor, even when it doesn't feel like it right away.

DAY 20:
I DON'T CHASE; I ATTRACT

My little sister taught me this lesson shortly after my divorce. I was back in the dating world, feeling uncomfortable and worried about why I was chasing all these men. One day, while recounting a story about a guy I was dating who started to ignore me, I felt awful. I really liked him and wanted to build a healthy relationship. But day in and day out, he kept pulling away. I didn't know what to do to change his mind. She listened and said, "Sissy, we don't chase; we attract."

Whether it's a relationship you are after or anything else in your life, having that mindset will shift your energy. You'll stop trying to control people or situations and simply attract the right people and situations to you.

Here's the trick: You must create the right type of energy to attract the right things and people to you. If you are negative, unkind, complaining, and overall depressed, it will be very difficult to attract positive situations into your life. The energy just won't line up. You attract what you are.

You must first get your energy right.

1. Evaluate your current energy. You can do this through journaling or talking about it. Ask yourself the question: how do I feel most of the time?

2. Recognize the people or things in your life that are draining your energy. Get rid of energy drainers or have a serious conversation about what you expect from them to be a part of your life. This seems harsh, but it's true.

3. Start a meditation practice. This will still your mind and recalibrate your energy.

4. Focus on the energy you want more of internally through your thoughts all day long. Do you want to be more loving? Have loving thoughts. Do you want to have more peace? Think about peaceful things. Do you want more fun? Think about fun things!

5. Give yourself grace. In this moment of change and focus, there are bound to be days that you are not in your best place. That's okay. Let it go and continue to try to build.

Evaluate your current energy. You can do this through journaling or talking about it. Ask yourself the question: how do I feel most of the time?

What is positive energy?

Positive energy is everything about an uplifting, encouraging, radiant vibe and attitude that brings on good feelings and situations. People with positive energy tend to be very present in their lives, radiating their beautiful energy in everything they do. You intuitively feel safe, happy, and relaxed around them. Their vibe is welcoming. You love being around them because, knowingly or not, you feed off those good vibes. Generosity, kindness, empathy, calm, optimism, and enthusiasm are all aspects of positive energy. Some people seem to access it naturally, while others must work harder to cultivate a positive outlook on life.[1]

What is negative energy? Negative energy means the so-called "off vibes." It refers to the moments and situations when you're feeling drained, tired, and uncomfortable. And the thing is, negative vibes are as contagious as positive vibes. Think of a time when you visited a friend who was having a hard time. Regardless of how you felt going into the encounter, you likely left feeling pretty bummed out. Negative people are judgmental, insecure, dissatisfied complainers, likely putting others down, and often all about doom and gloom. You intuitively feel insecure, unhappy, and tense around them. Their vibe is off-putting.[2]

---

[1]   by Jeffrey Allen, Alexandra Tudor
      https://blog.mindvalley.com/positive-and-negative-energy/
[2]   by Jeffrey Allen, Alexandra Tudor
      https://blog.mindvalley.com/positive-and-negative-energy/

The energy you bring to your life will impact every single area of your life. As you choose different energy, you will start to feel differently. Choosing to have a positive outlook on every area of your life is key to attracting new things into your life. Your high-vibe energy will automatically start to attract other high-vibe things into your life. I have a grandma who is focused on positive energy and brings it to every area of her life. She oozes positivity and fun light energy! She attracts relationships into her life because of this intentionality.

However, the opposite is true too. Negative energy can and will attract hard things into your life. I have a friend who is constantly negative. His outlook on life is blurred with negative thoughts. Unfortunately, this has caused him to have a lot of illness in his life. His body is sick because of all the negative thoughts he has. Negative thinking will not only stop all the good things from coming into your life, but it will also hurt your body in many ways.

Each day, you have a choice on what energy you want to fuel in your life. Positive energy or negative energy.

Recognize the people or things in your life that are drawing from your energy.

This is a hard truth. As you think about the people you spend the most time with, do they tend to be mostly positive or negative in their outlook on life? This is a big determinant of your happiness too. It's hard to be constantly lifting a negative person. It will eventually drain you.

If you want to have a positive life, it is key to surround yourself with positive people. I know we all go through hard things in life. So I am not saying to deny those things, but I am saying it is important to recognize if negativity is beginning to be a habit of thinking.

Start a meditation practice. This will still your mind and recalibrate your energy.

Starting a meditation practice will help you calm down your mind and emotions to become more centered. By giving your body space to be rather than do, you will see new parts of yourself emerge. I have found the Calm app has helped me a lot. I remember starting the practice and not being able to calm myself and my thoughts down enough to get through 3 minutes of meditation. Now I regularly do 10-minute sessions. The difference will be felt quickly.

Focus on the energy you want more of internally through your thoughts all day long.

Do you want to be more loving? Have loving thoughts. Do you want to have more peace? Think about peaceful things. Do you want more fun? Think about fun things! You are what you think.

One thing I did when I was trying to improve my thoughts is I would be an observer of my thoughts. All day long I would listen to my thoughts and classify them as loving or fear-based thoughts. I did not get upset with my fear-based thoughts; I would just observe them and let them go. I would intentionally think about loving thoughts and things. These thoughts made my entire heart and mind happy. Those loving thoughts would lead to new positive situations in my life. It is amazing how powerful our thoughts are!

Give yourself grace.

In this moment of change and focus, there are bound to be days that you are not in your best place. That's okay. Let it go and continue to try to build. It is difficult to make big changes in your life. Give yourself grace and space to learn how to cultivate a new way of living.

Each day, you have the power to attract new things into your life. Positive or negative. What do you choose?

DAY 21:
I WILL MAKE EVERYTHING
AROUND ME BEAUTIFUL

S pring has sprung in Wisconsin, and as I type this, the birds chirp outside my window. The leaves have burst open, the grass is a vibrant green, and flowers are popping up everywhere, signaling a fresh new start.

Reflecting on this time last year, I honestly didn't notice any of these things. It felt like a dark veil had been pulled over everything beautiful. Have you ever felt that?

I was grappling with the decision of whether to pursue a divorce, contemplating selling our dream home, and pondering where I would live and work. My mind was pulled in countless directions, overwhelmed by the weight of these decisions.

In that tumultuous period of my life, I realized I needed to trust my intuition and make some monumental decisions.

And so I did. I realized the relationship was beyond repair, and I needed a divorce. Our house, though beautiful, was too large and costly, necessitating its sale. I applied for jobs and began interviewing, eventually finding a lovely home for myself and my kids at the base of the mountain I loved to hike.

These decisions felt like the most daunting of my life because I knew they had the power to reshape not only my future but also that of my children.

It was a heavy burden to bear.

I turned to prayer and journaling to find clarity about what I needed to be happy again, and what I needed to feel peace, love, and joy.

In the simplest of terms, I decided: I will make everything around me beautiful. I will foster beautiful connections with my kids, with family, and with friends. I'll cultivate a serene, welcoming home filled with my favorite things. I'll nurture my mind with beautiful thoughts and create beautiful experiences. My entire life will be devoted to creating beauty. I knew this approach would work because I had glimpses of beauty in the past, but I had never been intentional about creating it.

I'm not sure what challenges you're facing in your life right now, but I do know this: if you focus on creating more beauty, you may be astonished by the results.

As I began intentionally curating beauty in my life, I found beautiful souls drawn to me. My friendships blossomed, conversations became richer, and my kids and I forged beautiful memories. Slowly but surely, the dark veil that had shrouded my life began to lift, and everything seemed more beautiful. Colors appeared brighter, laughter came easier, love flowed more freely, and I felt rejuvenated.

The more beauty we gather, the more we can give.

What if you directed your energy toward creating more beauty in your life? Imagine filling your life with so much beauty that it bursts at the seams! Seek out all the goodness you can.

DAY 22:
KEEP A GRATEFUL HEART

L ast night, around 9:30 pm, our relationship came to an end. Initially, I had high hopes for it, but over time, the imbalance became increasingly apparent. Eventually, I found myself as the sole contributor to the relationship, while he offered excuses for his lack of reciprocation.

When it ended, I experienced an overwhelming sense of relief and peace. It felt as though a heavy weight had been lifted from my entire being, allowing me to breathe freely once more. We parted ways with me professing my love and him bidding farewell. It was a classic scenario: I was always extending love, while receiving none in return.
I took a deep breath.

Lying in bed, I pondered how I could feel such immense relief. In fact, I even texted him to express my gratitude for ending it. Relief washed over me like a wave, and it felt as though angels were singing—Hallelujah.

Maintaining a grateful heart in the face of change or adversity requires intentionality. I thanked him for the time we shared and acknowledged the wonderful memories we created. However, I couldn't ignore the pain and hardships that also characterized our relationship. Unfortunately, they overshadowed the love we once had. Such is life, I suppose.

Gratitude has the power to reframe life's challenges. It allowed me to focus on the positive aspects and let go of the negative. I learned to appreciate his presence in my life while recognizing that it was not meant to be forever. It was merely a chapter in my life, not the entire story.

During my divorce, I realized that dwelling on the hardships could rob me of joy. So, I made a conscious effort to thank God every day for the blessings in my life: my children, family, friends, my dog, a good cup of coffee, laughter—everything. Gradually, the good began to outweigh the bad, and I found myself focusing more on the positive aspects of my life.

Gratitude shifts your perspective from what's wrong to what's right. Rather than dwelling on the pain, you focus on the blessings.

By repeatedly shifting your perspective, you train yourself to see the good in every situation. Even in the midst of a breakup, I found reasons to be grateful—for the beautiful moments we shared and the kindness we showed each other, especially in the end.

Take a moment to write down all the things that are going well in your life right now.

DAY 23:
GROW IN PATIENCE

I wish I could say I am a patient person, but I'm just not. It's like I'm missing that piece of me. If I want something, I want it now. If I want to do something, I want to do it now. If I have an idea, I implement it immediately.

In some respects, this can-do attitude is useful, especially because I am an entrepreneur at heart, and in business, you have to have this self-motivation.

However, in life, it can be hard to be patient when things are not going the way you want them to. In relationships, patience is key. In your health, patience helps you feel calmer. In everyday life, patience helps you navigate challenges with more grace.

Growing in patience takes time and effort.

I think the person I need to be the most patient with is myself. I need to give myself permission to slow down, to be more present, to allow myself to feel emotions, to rest if I need rest, to laugh if I need to laugh, and to ask for help. For me, patience is an all-day, every-day effort. It shows up in my thoughts. Am I being harsh and mean to myself, or am I being kind and patient? If I screw up, do I give myself grace and let it go, or do I ruminate on it?

Patience is a practice. Being patient with yourself in your challenges is a practice that will help you grow in wisdom and grace on a whole new level. If I think about some of the most understanding and patient people in my life, I think about older adults. Grandma Char has a calm patience in how she speaks, acts, and behaves. She doesn't get too bent out of shape about life. She has lived for 92 years and has seen and experienced so many things. When life throws her something, she goes with it. She lets it happen, and she patiently accepts it for what it is.

Patiently accepting life as it comes to you is a superpower. Letting life unfold and seeing it for what it is rather than what you want it to be is a true skill of growth. Can you let it flow? Can you witness the things happening and try not to place judgment on them? Better yet, can you trust that it is all working out exactly as it should?

I think being patient is a form of trusting that God will provide exactly what you need in your life when the timing is right. When you can fully and completely trust that every person, situation, and circumstance you need to have in your life is unfolding perfectly in alignment with what you need, then you will feel a whole new level of peace.

You will be able to wait patiently in your life, knowing the right people are going to enter at the right time. You will know that the hard or difficult thing you are experiencing will end at the right time. The resources will come to you.

I like to set the intention for what I want. Then I take action toward it, and I give it no tension. Patience will allow you to be fully and completely in the moment. Patience does not mean sitting around waiting for things to happen for you. I do believe that you need to work toward things in your life. You need to make an effort. You need to have goals and work on them.

But...

Once you have the vision for what you want, then you can patiently wait for it to unfold exactly how it should.

Grow in your patience. Grow in your trust. Grow in your ability to know that you are being guided toward the highest, most amazing version of your future!

DAY 24:
DON'T LOSE HOPE

Hope is my daughter's middle name. When I chose it, I knew I never wanted her to lose hope in life, and if she had it as her middle name, she would always have it be a part of who she was. I have found that having hope in my life has been one of the most powerful parts of living out my faith. I believe having hope has allowed me to look for a glimmer of good in the darkest of moments. I found myself searching for the lesson in the pain and hoping that tomorrow would be better.

Living in a constant state of hope allows you to have the lens that there is always something exciting to look forward to. There is always a brighter day on the horizon. Things will inevitably get better. Life will turn out okay.

Hope has taught me to:

- Believe even when I can't see the answer.
- Look for the lesson in pain.

- Strive to focus on the good daily.
- Understand that in time, things heal.

BELIEVE WHEN I CAN'T SEE THE ANSWER

For much of my life, I would focus on the things I didn't like, and I'd wonder why things were so bad. I'd ruminate in negative thinking day in and day out. I experienced anxiety and depression during these phases in my life because I would put all of my energy into all of the hard things I could not control and feel overwhelmed by negativity. When I lived in this way, it felt like I had a dark cloud following me everywhere I went. Bad stuff kept happening because that's all I could see happening. It was a terrible way to live.

Then one day, I wondered what would happen if I took the opposite approach. What if I looked for all of the good in my life and focused all of my attention and energy on it? What if I had an intention that everything was working out better than I could have imagined? At first, it felt like I was forcing this new attitude on my life. It felt awkward and weird to look for the good in every situation, even the really sucky ones. But eventually, this way of looking at life became a habit. Seeing the good became something I could see in most situations, if not immediately, pretty shortly afterward.

Believing when you can't see the answer allows you to feel hope that good things are aligning in your life. Imagine for a moment the things in your life that you feel are not working are actually gifts to bring you to a whole new place in your life. Believing the answer will arrive and lead you in the right direction is what hope is all about.

Another helpful strategy is to look for the lesson in pain. Sometimes life is hard and terrible! Sometimes what is happening seems unfair, and you may wonder why in the heck it is happening to you. It's okay to feel this way sometimes. I've found that even in that space, I try to ask myself what is the lesson I'm learning in my pain? If I reframe the pain to something I could teach others, then the pain I am going through makes more sense. In the last year, my pain has allowed me to truly appreciate the people in my life in a whole new way. It's made me stronger and more resilient. It's helped me know that I can navigate hard situations with grace. It's allowed me to slow down. It's taught me how to love. It's taught me how to ask for what I want. It's allowed me to be vulnerable. All of these lessons will help me parent in a new way. I'll be a better sister, daughter, and friend.

STRIVE TO FOCUS ON THE GOOD DAILY!

In the morning with my coffee and journal, I sit down and think about all of the good things happening in my life. My kids, my friends, my health

Understand that in time things heal
As I've been hurt the pain feels overwhelming to me. I want it to just go away. The healing process takes time. Think about the last cut you got. At first it stings and throbs. You feel uncomfortable and it hurts. Day by day you notice the cut less and less. The same happens with emotional pain.

At first the pain hurts so bad. You are in denial and shock and just want life to return to what you felt before the pain. You want to make it better. If it's a relationship you try to fix the pain and return to normal. And yet whatever pain happened was for a specific reason. Having hope that you will heal from the pain will allow you to take the process a day at a time. Allowing yourself to focus on what you need now and not too far in the future will let you heal.

Having more hope will change your life for the better. Always believing things are working out for your will change your perspective of hard things. Letting yourself lean the the belief that you an navigate hard things will give you hope. Hope will transform everything.

DAY 25:
DIVINE TIMING

W hat if everything in your life is happening at the exact right time and in the exact right way? Wouldn't that perspective help ease your mind about what is happening in your life right now?

In theory, yes. In practice, maybe not so much. I recently went through a breakup with a very wonderful person. We talked for months about our future and painted the perfect picture of how everything would fall into place. We dreamed. We did book studies about our passions. We loved each other deeper than either of us had ever experienced. Then, one day, it all shifted. The love, the deep connection, the fun, the lightness—gone. I tried to hold onto it, to locate it, but for some reason, it just evaporated.

My heart was broken. My mind could not comprehend what had happened. Thoughts swirled in my head about conversations we had and if I had said something wrong. I apologized. I gave him extra love. I showered him with support and words of affirmation. I tried all of the things to rekindle our love.

But in the end, it wasn't there anymore. And on the last conversation, I didn't even cry (I did many days before and after). I felt a weird sense of peace and relief when it was done.

I may never fully understand why that relationship had to end. I know that there must have been some reason it didn't work.

He came into my life during one of the hardest times of my life to offer a beautiful distraction. He was loving and kind. He shared experiences and fun. He was thoughtful, and we talked for hours. It was everything I wanted in a relationship. I believe when he came into my life was timed divinely to help me during a challenging time.

Then, as the hard things in my life were wrapping up and my confidence grew, our relationship withered. I felt more stable and calm in who I was, and then together, we did not feel as calm and in love. I honestly believe that happened at the exact right moment too.

Life flows. Sometimes things are all going exactly how you want them to. Sometimes they are not.

Sometimes you get a call, and the person on the other end says words you needed to hear at that exact moment. This is divine timing.

Or you run into an old friend at the exact right time to have a wonderful conversation that brings a new outlook on something you have been struggling with in your life.

Trusting that all of the things in your life are unfolding versus the feeling like you need to push/control things will give you peace. I like to say that everything is working out for me and it will be better than I could have imagined. The people, the resources, the ideas, the opportunities are all aligning for my highest good. If that is true then I know I can relax with calm confidence that I am being divinely guided.

Today, think back to all of the times in your life when things just fell into place for you. You got the right job. You found the right outfit. You met the right person. You read the right book. You had the right conversation. These moments, one by one, will make up the fabric of your life. When you can trust in the fact that you are being guided and everything is aligned in divine timing, it will give you peace and trust.

DAY 26:
LET IT GO/SELF RESPECT

L ife doesn't always unfold as planned. Relationships falter, illness strikes, jobs evaporate, homes must be sold, and dreams crumble. Sometimes, it feels as though nothing is going right, and you find yourself wondering what's happening.

I've been there too. I remember when I separated from my husband, initiated divorce proceedings, packed up a household, readied it for sale, searched for a new car, hunted for a job, secured a rental, and amidst it all, sought to rediscover myself.

Within 6-9 months, everything in my life underwent a complete transformation. I became divorced, inhabited a different home, drove a different car, pursued a different occupation, carried a different surname, and found myself surrounded by different friends.

Letting go of my former life seemed unimaginable. Initially, I clung to the dreams and hopes I had for our family and our rekindled relationship. I'm an optimist, perhaps to a fault. I have a knack for finding goodness in the bleakest situations, a glimmer of hope amidst chaos. This optimism, in many ways, shielded me and bolstered my resilience. However, it also led me to ignore harsh realities—the abuse festering in my marriage, the daily struggles my children and I endured, the darkness enveloping me. I couldn't keep pretending that none of it existed. I needed to confront it, to acknowledge its weight.

Facing reality head-on is brutal. Being brutally honest about life's challenges can feel like a gut punch. Accepting the harsh truths and deciding to let go is one of the most daunting and courageous acts I've undertaken.

Let it go!
Let it go!
Let it go!

Moving beyond pain entails gradually releasing it. I had to recognize it for what it was: a toxic, abusive relationship incompatible with my growth.

I consciously chose to let it go. If it were meant for me, it wouldn't inflict pain. If it were meant for me, I wouldn't have to struggle incessantly. If it were meant for me, my heart wouldn't ache daily. If it were meant for me, I wouldn't dread each waking moment.

Let it go!

Three words with immense power to transform life. At times, I had to relinquish the visions or dreams I harbored for that relationship. Just because I envisioned them didn't guarantee their reality. Perhaps they were never meant to materialize, or perhaps they were meant to manifest with someone else.

During a recent mountain hike with a close friend, I pondered a concept: self-respect.

I realized I must respect myself enough to cease chasing those who don't reciprocate. It's painful to accept rejection from someone you deeply love. Yet, I found the strength to acknowledge my worthiness of profound love. I am extraordinary, and the right person wouldn't push me away.

Self-respect is acknowledging your worthiness. It's recognizing your inherent power. It's allowing your heart to believe that if one door closes, a more beautiful one will open. Even when your desired outcomes crumble, they might be paving the way for a new, love-filled, supportive, and joyous chapter.

To be honest, I'm still navigating these lessons daily. I'm still holding onto the life I once envisioned, still in the process of healing. I wish healing followed a linear path. I wish there were a checklist by my bedside, guiding me through daily tasks to mend my broken heart. But healing is more akin to scar tissue—visible reminders of past pain. The wounds close, but the scars remain, serving as a testament to the resilience within us.

We all bear scars, endure pain, confront inexplicable hardships. Yet, we can't dwell on the "whys" or "hows." All we can do is let go and muster enough self-respect to forge ahead, crafting a new life.

Today, I urge you to compile a list of things to release from your life—be it limiting beliefs or hindrances. Contemplate how liberating yourself from these burdens will feel. That act of letting go is an act of self-respect. It's recognizing that you deserve more—more love, more support, more laughter, more kindness, more of life's bounty. You deserve it all!

DAY 28:
MAGIC IS BELIEVING IN YOURSELF

When was the last time you looked at yourself in the mirror and truly honored the amazing person you are? When did you last feel awed by your own strength and beauty?

If it hasn't been recently, then I'm granting you permission to embark on the magical journey of believing in yourself.

I have an embarrassing secret: for most of my life, I compared myself to others. I spent too much time striving to become a different version of myself.

DAY 29:
BUILD THE NEW

T here are moments in life when we can no longer continue with the status quo. We must toss our comfort zone out the window and embrace the process of building something new!

For much of my life, I resisted change and did everything in my power to avoid it. I lingered in relationships past their expiration dates, resided in the wrong areas for too long, and engaged in activities that failed to bring me joy.

Why did I get stuck? Because familiarity breeds comfort. Sometimes, it's easier to remain in an uncomfortable situation than to venture into the unknown and unfamiliar. For many of us, the prospect of the unknown is daunting; we fear it might lead to unfavorable outcomes.

But here's the revelation I've had: that which is new and intimidating might just be the key to your happiness and excitement! Change has the potential to bring peace and joy into your life.

Trust that change enters your life precisely when you need it to facilitate your growth.

When I embark on building something new, I find a quiet spot and brainstorm all the wonderful things I want in the life I'm creating: a tranquil home, a vibrant community, the laughter of children, security, cherished friends and family, abundant love and happiness, meaningful conversations, and robust health.

As I embark on this journey, I remind myself to focus on the things I truly desire and to invest all my energy into manifesting them. I must become fully immersed in bringing these desires into my reality, nurturing excitement and anticipation for their arrival. And when they do materialize, I take the time to celebrate them.

Too often, we find ourselves fixating on what's missing in our lives—the things we long for but haven't yet attained. We spend hours lamenting failed relationships or unsuccessful job interviews, dwelling on what hasn't worked out instead of appreciating what has. Consider that those disappointments may have been blessings in disguise, safeguarding you from heartache or dissatisfaction.

When I ponder why certain things haven't worked out in my life, I remind myself that what is meant for me will always find its way to me—always! I need not exert control or force; the right people, resources, and opportunities will naturally gravitate toward me. And in that knowledge, I find solace, knowing that I needn't worry about when they'll arrive; all I need to do is trust that they are coming.

The beauty of surrendering my plans is that it opens the door to unexpected synchronicities. A chance conversation may lead me to the car I've been eyeing, or a simple chat with a friend might pave the way to a new relationship. A quick online search might reveal the perfect place to live, or a spontaneous road trip might unveil the ideal coffee spot.

As I've learned to surrender, my Type A tendencies have relaxed. I've come to understand that while I can't control everything in my life, I can clarify what I want and take steps to create it.

DAY 30:
LAUGHTER AND SLEEP: THE ULTIMATE REMEDIES!

L ast night, I slept soooo well. I went to bed early because I hadn't been sleeping well, and I simply drifted off. I woke up early, without needing my alarm, and my whole body felt refreshed.

When was the last time you experienced that kind of rest? The rejuvenating, incredible, body-resetting kind? If it's been a while, schedule some time to make it happen.

After a good night's rest, I feel like a new person. The problems that plagued me yesterday seem to dissolve. My fears diminish, and my heart feels fuller. I'm more patient with my kids, and I'm more productive at work. Overall, sleep makes all the difference.

Dr. Maiken Nedergaard, who studies sleep at the University of Rochester, says, "While you sleep, your brain is working.

For example, sleep helps prepare your brain to learn, remember, and create."

This is why after a great night's rest, you feel better overall and probably get more done!

For many years, I limited my nightly sleep. I'd stay up late, get woken up by one of my kids, and then wake up early. Day in and day out, I was exhausted. Then, I went through life changes, and I focused on sleep as part of my healing process. I learned to go to bed earlier and wake up later. I made sure the kids knew they could not sleep with me. All this led me to finally get a full eight hours of sleep, and it was glorious. After all that sleep, my brain was sharper. I could make decisions more easily. I could physically accomplish more. I was happier and more peaceful. Overall, sleep made all the difference.

Many people try to limit their sleep and feel like they don't have time to rest. In my healing process, I've found sleep to be a game-changer. I think if I had tried to heal without sleep, I would have failed miserably. I might have lasted for a little while, but eventually, the lack of sleep would have caught up to me, and my healing would have crumbled quickly.

The other part of this process is laughter! I try to laugh every single day. For a while, I was looking up funny animal videos to chuckle at. There were cats "driving" cars and other silly animals to giggle at. It was forced laughter, but it made me feel happier. It's hard to have a bad day when you're laughing.

The other day, as I packed up my kids and our stuff to leave my parents' cabin, I sat down, ready to go, and realized I'd forgotten my dog in the cabin with my parents! I laughed soooo hard. Find little things to laugh about. Find silly things your kids do to laugh about. Think about funny things to laugh about. Journal about the things that make you laugh. Just laugh!

Laughter is like a miracle worker when it comes to healing. When I started college, I was having a hard time transitioning, and I received a card from my mom. It said, "Life is too short to be serious!" It was right. I was taking myself too seriously. I was looking at life through a lens of seriousness, which blurred everything into being hard and challenging. Life has its serious aspects, for sure, but if you can find laughter and happiness in the hard times, it makes it much easier to get through.

Your priorities today are laughter + sleep = happiness and healing!

DAY 31:
REFLECT ON THE STRENGTH YOU'VE GAINED!

Y ou are stronger than you realize. I can't count how many times people have reminded me of this.

The truth is, when I was facing some of the toughest challenges in my life, I didn't feel strong at all. But I had no choice. I had to confront the difficulty, work through it, and figure things out. Over and over, as hardships continued to arise, I realized I couldn't hide from the problems—I had to face them head-on.

Strength isn't cultivated during life's easy moments. It's forged when we're knocked down and muster the courage to get back up, time and time again. Strength is showing up for yourself, honoring your emotions, and moving forward regardless. Strength is learning to say no, stepping away from toxic relationships, and embracing new experiences.

True strength is found when you confront your deepest fears head-on and push through them. It's waking up one day with the inner resolve to move forward despite confusion.

My divorce boosted my confidence to navigate life independently and build a new future for myself and my children. My job taught me that I was capable and employable. Witnessing my health improve showed me that by slowing down and nurturing my body, transformation was possible.

Every trial and tribulation in life offers a lesson. This past year, I've learned so much about how I handle challenges. My strength to advocate for myself has grown, as has my ability to show up and leave situations that no longer serve me.

Quitting isn't always a negative thing. Ending a toxic relationship can be one of the bravest decisions you'll ever make. Breaking free from negative thinking can revolutionize how you engage with life. Ditching unhealthy habits can fortify your body and mind. Walking away from a job that drains you can bring peace and happiness. In our culture, quitting is often viewed negatively, but I see it as one of the strongest choices you can make. Consider all the people who remain trapped in broken relationships, unfulfilling jobs, or harmful habits simply because they lack the strength to quit.

What's the top thing you need to quit in your life right now? Why is quitting this thing important to you? What will it mean to stop doing it?

Strength emerges from being brutally honest with yourself about what you need to cultivate more happiness in your life.

Are you content in your relationships?
Do you feel valued and fulfilled in your job?
Are you satisfied with your health and well-being?

Examine the key areas of your life and be honest with yourself. If you find yourself answering no to any of these questions, it's time to summon your strength. It's time to prioritize yourself and make bold changes!

DAY 32:
YES, YOU CAN!

Too often, I find myself feeding my fears and doubts. I dwell on all the things I can't do rather than focusing on what I can do. I fixate on my weaknesses instead of embracing my strengths. Day in and day out, I chip away at my confidence by constantly dwelling on what might go wrong or what I might fail at.

My friend Sarah runs a fitness company called "Yes, You Can!" Three simple words that can shift your doubts. Three words that can empower you to try new things or pursue that dream career. Three words that can inspire you to bet on your abilities and trust that you'll figure it out.

To identify the things I needed most in my life, I decided to confront my fears head-on. I wrote down 10 things I was afraid of right now:

1. Finding a hobby I'm passionate about.
2. Letting go of love.

3. Being a single mom.
4. Publishing this book.
5. Going on a solo trip. Being alone.
6. Never being able to buy a house.
7. Pain from the past.
8. Never finding love.
9. Never feeling financially secure.
10. Not being able to provide for my kids.

I share these 10 fears because we all have them. We all have things we're afraid to try, afraid to do, afraid to face. Fears reside within all of us.

The thing about fears is, once you identify them, you can recognize what you need to pursue. Fears are the signposts pointing you toward growth. You fear something because deep down, you know you need it.

The next step is to FLIP your fears into "Yes, You Can" statements by taking one small action toward each fear:

1. Finding a hobby I'm passionate about > start researching fun activities.
2. Letting go of love > move forward with my life.
3. Being a full-time single mom > ask for help from family and friends.
4. Publishing this book > begin the publishing process.
5. Going on a solo trip. Being alone > explore potential travel destinations.
6. Never being able to buy a house > remain open to potential home options.

7. Pain from the past > refuse to let past mistakes define you.
8. Never finding love > acknowledge that love is within reach.
9. Never feeling financially secure > seek guidance from financial professionals.
10. Not being able to provide for my kids > trust in your ability to always find a way.

See how taking one small step toward facing our fears can transform them into manageable challenges? After confronting my own fears in this way, I felt empowered. Instead of letting fears consume me, they became catalysts for empowerment in my life. Fears often hold us back from living the life we desire. They keep us awake at night and hinder our progress. But when we turn our fears into actionable steps, we strip them of their power over us.

YES, YOU CAN!
You can rewrite the narrative you tell yourself. You can transform your fears into opportunities for growth. You can choose to let your mind dwell on fear or move forward with purpose.

YOU CAN!
For too long, I resisted change and dwelled on all the negative possibilities in my life. But as I began to confront my fears and take small steps forward, I realized I had far more control over my life than I had believed. I was the one in charge of feeding my fears or fueling my faith. By choosing to feed my faith, I reclaimed my power. I took control of my destiny. And you can do the same!

DAY 33:
GROWTH

Wouldn't it be wonderful if growth happened effortlessly, amidst a backdrop of ease and smooth sailing? We'd simply evolve and progress to the next version of ourselves. Happy unicorns would prance about, butterflies would flutter, and birds would sing on a scorching summer day.

But the truth is, growth requires confronting tough challenges and actively choosing to learn and evolve from those experiences.

In my own journey of growth, I found myself thrust into situations I desperately wanted to avoid. It's tempting to turn a blind eye to unhealthy behaviors or pretend that abuse doesn't exist. It's easy to gloss over loveless relationships or low self-worth if you convince yourself that everything is fine.

But eventually, something shifts, and reality comes crashing in. The deception, hurt, and pain resurface. When this happened in my life, I felt disoriented and terrified. The unknown loomed before me like Mount Everest, daunting and overwhelming. I felt utterly unprepared, scared witless, and clueless about where to begin.

In that abyss of uncertainty and confusion, I began rebuilding our lives. Day by day, I tackled the chaos, sought help, and focused on growth. I realized that to forge a new path, I had to release the grip of the past entirely. I couldn't cling to any shred of what our life used to be.

Letting go of the past proved arduous. I had been coasting through life on autopilot, clinging to routines and comforts, even if they were detrimental. But to grow, I had to confront the upheaval and decide which pieces of my old life to salvage and which to discard.

I realized there were many things I could let go of. To foster growth for myself and my children, we prioritized the essentials and shed the rest. We worked tirelessly to rebuild our hearts and minds, preparing for the growth that life had in store.

Each of us experienced growth differently. Some days were marked by tears, while others overflowed with exhaustion and overwhelm. But amidst the chaos, there were also moments of embrace and laughter.

Life's growth isn't linear; it's messy and demanding. It requires time, patience, resilience, and the courage to set boundaries and say no.

And at the end of that tumultuous journey, you emerge as a different version of yourself. I became Allison 2.0, unrecognizable to those who knew me before. It was a testament to my commitment to growth, to honoring my truth, and letting go of the past.

Find that unwavering determination within yourself. Refuse to let anything or anyone hinder your pursuit of a new life. NO ONE!

Get your mindset in alignment.
Get your body moving.
Seek assistance when needed.
Wake up each day ready to take one step toward becoming the new version of yourself.
And one day, you'll awaken with peace and love in your heart. You'll gaze upon your new surroundings, with newfound love and countless blessings, and realize that every ounce of pain you endured was worth it. Every tear shed, every doubt faced, every fear conquered—all were worth it. That, my friend, is why growth is essential!

DAY 34:
FIND MORE FUN

Yesterday, I awoke in a state of panic. It felt as though a heavy weight rested on my chest. My heart was heavy, and I felt lost.

I faced a choice:

1. Sit in my sadness and wallow in self-pity.
2. Throw on my running gear and join my friend for a 5k.

Either choice could have sufficed, but despite my inner resistance, I opted for the latter. I went through the motions, dressing myself and heading out for a run with my friend and her daughter. It took a few moments, but gradually, I began to feel lighter. The burden lifted as I listened to my friend's stories and let go of my own worries.

By the end of the race, I felt whole again. My heart danced with joy, and I faced the day with renewed vigor.

I found fun! It wasn't a necessity, but it made all the difference. After the run, I tackled a slew of chores before meeting my friend for tacos—an added dose of fun. Then, we spent the afternoon floating at the beach on colorful inflatables, laughing and chatting for hours. It was pure bliss!

By the time I returned home, my heart overflowed with happiness. Fun had worked its magic once again. Sometimes, amidst life's challenges, we convince ourselves that fun is a luxury we cannot afford. But in reality, it's during these difficult times that we need fun the most. We must actively seek out joy and happiness, knowing that we deserve it.

So, how can you find more fun when life feels tough?

First, grant yourself permission to have fun. It may seem counterintuitive during difficult times, but fun is always allowed! Laughter and joy can provide a fresh perspective and reinvigorate your spirit.

Next, seek out simple pleasures. Look for something fun you can do today, whether it's spending time with a friend, taking a leisurely walk, or watching a funny movie. Fun doesn't have to be elaborate; it just needs to bring you joy.

Once you've had your first taste of fun, you'll be hooked!

Finally, create a list of fun activities you'd like to experience. Whether it's exploring new places, trying new hobbies, or simply enjoying the season's offerings, keep your eyes open for opportunities to add to your list.

Fun is an essential part of life. It enriches our experiences and rejuvenates our souls. Embrace fun, and let it transform your healing journey, providing moments of joy and respite amidst life's challenges.

DAY 35:
BE THANKFUL

L ife offers countless blessings to be thankful for, but it often requires intentional effort to recognize them. Once you start looking, you'll be amazed at the abundance of blessings surrounding you.

For the past few weeks, I've been feeling out of sorts. Each day seemed to be consumed by thoughts of sorrow and longing.

But yesterday, something shifted. I woke up with a sense of lightness, my heart unburdened. Throughout the day, I focused on activities that brought joy and fulfillment. I let go of the past, and it was liberating! I drove to my son's lacrosse game, basking in my favorite tunes. I spent time floating on a lake, engrossed in a good book. Setting up my new hammock, taking a nap, and hiking—all these acts of self-care helped me realize how much I had neglected my own needs in the relationship. While I had poured all my energy into making the other person happy, I had overlooked my own happiness.

I was grateful for this shift in perspective. Reflecting on my old journal entries about the relationship, I realized the depth of hurt I had been suppressing.

Sometimes, I tend to see the good in situations to a fault, and this relationship was no exception.

Stepping away from it, I acknowledged the pain it caused and recognized that it wasn't sustainable in the long run for either of us.

I'm thankful for the time we shared, but I'm also thankful to be free of it now.

Being thankful acknowledges the transient nature of people, opportunities, and experiences in our lives. Some stay, while others depart. We must appreciate their presence while they're here and gracefully let them go when it's time.

As I floated on the lake, I watched the waves ebb and flow. It struck me that life is much like these waves—constantly in motion. We must learn to go with the flow, allowing things to come and go as they please.

I have a tendency to cling tightly to my ideas and visions, believing that they must all come to fruition. But I've come to realize that not every vision is meant to manifest. And that's perfectly okay.

Being thankful, even when things don't go as planned, may seem counterintuitive. But I firmly believe that what's meant for us will find its way into our lives, while what isn't meant to be will naturally fade away.

Trust in the process of life. Trust in yourself. Trust that everything is unfolding as it should.

I often remind myself, "God is always conspiring for my highest good." This belief allows me to surrender to the flow of life, knowing that better things are on the horizon.

Similarly, I embrace the mantra, "Things always work out better than I could have imagined." This helps me release attachments to outcomes and accept that what's meant for me will manifest effortlessly.

The secret lies in relinquishing control and embracing presence. While we can't force people to stay or opportunities to materialize, we can find solace in being fully present and embracing each moment with excitement.

Today, I encourage you to reflect on what you're thankful for. Focus on the blessings in your life, no matter how small, and watch as they multiply.

DAY 36:
PERSPECTIVE CHANGES LIFE

H ave you ever found yourself firmly believing one thing, only to realize later that you were completely mistaken, leaving you feeling bewildered? I think we've all experienced this at some point, and it can indeed feel disorienting!

One of the most effective ways I illustrate the transformative power of perspective is by likening it to riding in a hot air balloon. When you're on the ground, everything appears clear and close at hand. But as the balloon ascends, a sense of awe washes over you as your perspective shifts. The familiar sights below seem distant, and you're enveloped by a vast expanse of sky and earth. The higher you go, the more expansive your view becomes, evoking feelings of wonder and excitement.

Changing your perspective can feel just as exhilarating.

Recently, I've had to shift my perspective on various aspects of my life. Initially, parenting as a single parent seemed overwhelming, but now it feels peaceful and manageable. Finding a safe place to live and packing up my old house for a move felt like daunting tasks, but now I'm settled into my new home comfortably and starting a business. Landing a job seemed like an insurmountable challenge until one day, it happened. And finding a deeply fulfilling relationship, once deemed impossible, suddenly materialized.

There are always aspects of life that appear daunting or unattainable. But then, through a shift in perspective, the answers seem to manifest almost magically, filling us with excitement and anticipation.

In my own healing journey, I've learned to release to the universe the things I have no control over. I identify my desires and intentions, take action toward them, and then release them with a sense of openness and curiosity.

Intention leads to action, which in turn leads to manifestation, without the burden of tension.

I've found that when I try to force or control outcomes, they often elude me. However, I'm willing to fight for the things that truly matter to me.

What matters most to you in life? Don't give up on those things. If there's a person or situation that persists in your thoughts, there's a reason for it. Embrace it, take action, and allow it to flow into your life.

Changing perspective also involves seeking understanding from others. Sometimes, situations defy logic, and we're left with a barrage of negative thoughts and self-blame.

In the journey of healing, sometimes we must have difficult conversations we'd rather avoid. We must approach them with openness, seeking to understand rather than judge. By truly listening to the perspectives of others, we can free ourselves from self-imposed limitations and move forward with clarity and grace.

DAY 37:
TRUST

M y word for this year is TRUST. As each year comes to a close, I seek guidance from God on the word I should focus on for the following year. This time, the word that resonated with me repeatedly was TRUST.

Trusting hasn't come easily for me. Whether it's trusting in God, trusting others, or trusting myself, it's been a journey filled with challenges.

I've often had to rely solely on myself to navigate through life. Growing up, I internalized the belief that if something needed to be done, I had to do it myself. This mindset led me to build walls around myself, shielding me from potential hurt and pain. But in doing so, I also prevented myself from forming genuine connections and authentic relationships.

Another significant challenge I faced was trusting in God. Surrendering my plans and allowing God's plans to unfold seemed daunting. I needed to learn to ask for help when life felt overwhelming and to let go of the need to control every aspect of my life. This shift towards placing my trust fully in God's love and guidance was not easy, especially since I had always believed that I was in control of my destiny.

Yet, little by little, I began to trust. I listened to my intuition, allowing God to illuminate my path. I sought God's guidance in making important decisions and trusted that He would lead me to where I needed to be. Whether it was welcoming new people into my life or bidding farewell to others, I trusted in God's divine plan. Even the small nudges, like reaching out to a friend or taking time to rest, became acts of trust in God's wisdom.

But let's be real—trust is hard work!

For someone like me, who thrives on control and planning, relinquishing that control was a significant challenge. I had to let go of my carefully crafted plans and be open to new possibilities. Embracing uncertainty and relinquishing control over my life felt uncomfortable and unfamiliar.

So, what happens when we trust?

When I release my grip on control and trust that God is guiding me, I relinquish the need to manipulate outcomes. I can't simply pray for help and then attempt to micromanage the situation. Instead, I must accept God's guidance and trust in His divine timing.

To embark on this journey of trust, I began by identifying the areas of my life that I was trying to control:

- My faith
- My family
- My relationships
- My health
- My finances
- My friendships

Then, I explored ways to release control and trust the process:

- Trusting my faith meant surrendering to God's will and seeking His guidance in all matters.
- Trusting my family involved letting go of the need to control their actions and allowing our relationships to evolve naturally.
- Trusting my relationships required accepting that some connections may not endure and believing that everything happens for a reason.
- Trusting my health meant prioritizing self-care and nurturing my physical and mental well-being.
- Trusting my finances involved adopting an abundance mindset and believing that my needs would be provided for.
- Trusting my friendships meant fostering open communication, offering support, and allowing space for growth.

Trusting in life's journey represents a profound shift. It's about acknowledging that much of what we try to control is ultimately beyond our grasp. Trusting that everything unfolds as it should is a powerful spiritual practice—one that opens us up to love, abundance, and endless possibilities.

So, trust that everything is working out in your favor. Embrace the uncertainty, knowing that what awaits you is far greater than anything you could have imagined!

DAY 38:
ACCEPTANCE/THIS IS
HOW IT IS NOW

When things don't turn out as you hoped, how do you react? I'll be honest... I cling on for dear life. I try to hold onto the person, thing, or opportunity because I find comfort in its presence in my life. What would my life be without them? Who would I become?

Life is in a constant state of change and flux. Whether I like it or not, people will enter and exit our lives. Circumstances will change. Opportunities will shift.

At times, it may feel unjust to let go of what we've grown accustomed to in order to embrace something new. But that's part of life. Acceptance is part of life. Acknowledging the new reality of our lives is a crucial step we must take.

Unfortunately, many people—myself included—cling onto relationships or ideals for far too long. We dwell in the past, holding onto what the relationship once meant to us and attempting to recreate it in the present.

One phrase a friend taught me for moments like these is, "This is how it is now." This simple yet profound phrase serves as a reminder to acknowledge that life changes, and in this moment, this is our reality. It's not what it was before, and we can't control what it will be in the future. All we can do is live in the present—today. Whatever it looks like today is what it is. This is our new reality.

Accepting the present moment can be challenging, but accepting life's changes is empowering. Allowing ourselves to fully embrace what life is now and being okay with it is a journey each of us should embark upon.

Often, what keeps us trapped in the cycle of trying to control our lives is the belief that things should remain the same. Life is dynamic and ever-evolving. The circumstances of our lives are bound to change, especially as we grow.

Trusting the process of life unfolding is powerful. Accepting that everything happening is ultimately for our good, even if it feels difficult in the moment, grounds us in the present reality. We are here, now. We cannot dwell in the past or predict the future. We cannot control how things unfold. Our task is simply to embrace today. Seek out the hidden treasures that each day brings. If thoughts of the past surface, try to let them go. If worries about the future arise, release them. Be fully present today. Accept whatever this day brings. In acceptance lies hope, clarity, and love. This is how it is now.

DAY 39:
LOVE

I am love. I am light. I am.

Loving yourself comes first. Before you can genuinely love others, you must find love within yourself. You can pretend to love others, but eventually, that facade will crumble. You must love who you are and be kind to yourself before you can authentically give love to others. You cannot pour from an empty cup. You cannot love from an empty heart.

I vividly recall the moment my children were born. The first time I held them, my heart overflowed with love. An overwhelming surge of affection enveloped us, and I knew my heart would forever be intertwined with theirs. Leaving my son with a nanny for the first time to go to work at the library brought tears to my eyes because being away from him felt like losing a part of myself, like losing an arm. Thankfully, I overcame that feeling, allowing him the independence to venture from my side, but initially, it was overwhelming.

One of the greatest challenges of love is when you offer it to someone, and it is unreciprocated or rejected. No matter how loving and kind you are, it may not be enough. Attempting to love someone who does not return that love can leave you feeling drained.

Recently, I experienced both divorce and a breakup, each carrying its own unique pain. The divorce hurt because it revealed how long I had denied myself happiness by remaining in a loveless marriage. The breakup hurt because I felt genuinely loved, only to have it come to an end.

Being open to loving another is vulnerable. We all instinctively shield our hearts to avoid pain. Some may spend their lives protecting their hearts or cautiously opening them only to quickly shut them again.

Begin by loving yourself completely. Recognize the gifts you possess and the love you offer to those around you. Look into the mirror and affirm, "I love you." Compile a list of ways to demonstrate self-love. Treat yourself with kindness and tenderness. Prioritize yourself. Extend grace and compassion to yourself. Practice self-care. Seek assistance in healing your wounds and traumas. Nourish your physical, emotional, and spiritual well-being. Chronicle your days in a journal. Engage in prayer frequently. Surround yourself with loving individuals.

The journey toward self-love may take time, but dedicating yourself daily to overcome your fears and nurture your faith will be rewarding. Investing time to mend your heart will yield peace. Embracing self-love fully will draw more love into your life.

It's often said that hurt people hurt people. I believe that loving people love people. Be a beacon of love in a fractured world. Prioritize yourself first. Love yourself first. In doing so, you will exemplify true love to your family, friends, and everyone you encounter. Eventually, the love you seek will be drawn to your loving spirit.

DAY 40:
CELEBRATE!

4 0 days of healing, 40 days of growth, 40 days of recognizing strength!

Today, I'm celebrating 40 days!!

40 days ago, I embarked on this journey on my 40th Birthday. I had no clue if I could do it or what it would become.

During these 40 days, I learned a lot about my resilience and strength. I was tested in my faith, felt deep hurt and pain, experienced overwhelming joy, and found peace, happiness, and love.

In 40 days, I truly lived. Day by day, I navigated life uncertain of its outcome. I endeavored to share my healing process, even rediscovering how to heal after a difficult time in my own life. Sometimes, you have to experience pain while walking through the writing process to authentically share it. Well, friends, I had the chance to authentically share pain. I would have preferred to draw from past experiences of pain, but that's how it unfolded.

I want to celebrate this milestone because when we express excitement and celebrate achievements in our lives, we signal to the universe that we desire more of those positive experiences!

Curious about how I'm marking this momentous occasion of writing this book? I'm finally embarking on my freedom trip to Seattle, WA. After my divorce, a friend suggested I take a solo trip to enjoy myself and reflect. I intended to do it last fall, but then I entered another relationship, lost myself, and learned some invaluable life lessons... and now, here I am! ☺

I will celebrate my strength, courage, and resilience. I'll rejoice in overcoming hardships, liberating myself from toxic relationships, and cherishing the beautiful souls around me. I'll revel in my vitality and celebrate myself.

You too can celebrate your journey. Acknowledge the difficult and beautiful days alike. Reflect on everything you've endured and conquered! Recognize your power, beauty, and capacity for love. Envision the incredible possibilities your future holds.

Celebrate!

On my freedom trip, my goal is simple: to have fun, enjoy myself, explore, laugh, savor coffee and delicious food, honor my journey, embrace the woman I've become, and simply be me.

Freedom is defined as the power or right to act, speak, or think as one wants without hindrance or restraint.

Imagine the exquisite feeling of freedom! Pure energy and love coursing through you. Granting yourself the permission to do, be, and have all that you desire.

Celebrate the new life you are creating!!!

THANK YOU!

Thank you to everyone who supported me and my kids during our healing journey. We feel blessed to be surrounded by some of the most amazing friends and family.

To anyone who is reading this book that is on their own healing journey I hope you find the courage to heal. You deserve a life of love and peace. You deserve happiness. You are loved.

Allison is available for speaking, coaching, consulting, and welcomes new awesome friendships from all over the world! Feel free to connect with her through her website: www. launchsuccess.co

Made in the USA
Monee, IL
20 March 2025

14335206R00079